Reflections

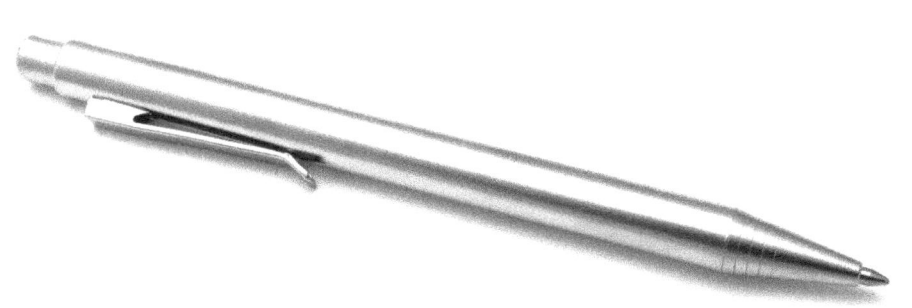

Reflections

a memoir

Robin Beazley

The Book Guild Ltd

First published in Great Britain in 2017 by
The Book Guild Ltd
9 Priory Business Park
Wistow Road, Kibworth
Leicestershire, LE8 0RX
Freephone: 0800 999 2982
www.bookguild.co.uk
Email: info@bookguild.co.uk
Twitter: @bookguild

Copyright © 2017 Robin Beazley

The right of Robin Beazley to be identified as the author of this
work has been asserted by him in accordance with the
Copyright, Design and Patents Act 1988.

All rights reserved. No part of this publication may be
reproduced, transmitted, or stored in a retrieval system, in any form or by any means,
without permission in writing from the publisher, nor be otherwise circulated in
any form of binding or cover other than that in which it is published and without
a similar condition being imposed on the subsequent purchaser.

Typeset in Minion Pro

Printed and bound in Great Britain by CPI Group (UK) Ltd, Croydon, CR0 4YY

ISBN 978 1912083 831

British Library Cataloguing in Publication Data.
A catalogue record for this book is available from the British Library.

This book is dedicated to all those persons, living or no longer with us, who are mentioned herein. Without them, this work could not have been written.

My memory of them is now set in print for all time.

Prologue

A wise man once said "If you have nothing to say, keep quiet or be prepared to make a fool of yourself".

I have had experiences in my life that I think are worth sharing. I am putting pen to paper in the hope that someone else in this world finds them interesting and, at times, dramatic and even amusing. I have tried to refrain from using persons' surnames and in the most have referred to them by their first names. On very few occasions I have avoided both to protect those persons who may feel aggrieved at having been mentioned. Nevertheless, I have attempted to refrain from fabricating and embellishing my account of the events I will place on record in this autobiography. I expect some people might feel I have been too candid.

Should I make a fool of myself, so be it. Better to have loved and lost, than etc. etc.

This autobiography has not been written on a strictly chronological timescale. I have grouped my writings in order, to co-ordinate my thoughts on different topics which I hope will make them more cohesive and interesting. This will also allow the reader the opportunity of skipping chapters they may consider to be of little interest.

Because of this I will now detail in brief a summary of Rhodesia during the years I lived there. I arrived in the country in April 1957. At that time the country was known as Southern

Rhodesia and formed a federation with Northern Rhodesia and Nyasaland. Sir Roy Welensky was the head of the government of the day. Salisbury was the capital city and it was in Salisbury that my family had taken up residence. My stepfather and his brothers were continuing their civil engineering business and constructed a couple of apartment blocks. One of these was the first in the country to let the apartments fully furnished. The demand for these apartments was considerable and all apartments were sold well before construction of the building had been completed.

The brothers had adopted a lifestyle which embraced equal time devoted to 'play' as to work. On completing a project, they would take time off (usually several months) and would only start another project when they considered the bank balance needed replenishing.

So successful were the constructions in Rhodesia, that once again the brothers sold up and retired; this time for good. They left Africa for Europe and I found myself 'homeless' in 1959.

In the early sixties, the Federation collapsed and Ian Smith became the prime minister of Southern Rhodesia until the 11th of November 1965 when he declared UDI (Unilateral Declaration of Independence).

I am surprised how often the date '11th day of the 11th month' has significance on monumental historical occasions. Twice, this day has meaning for me. I have mentioned Rhodesia's turning point in history. Also on this day in 1955, my present wife, Wendy, was born. Armistice Day in 1918 is probably the one that had most affect on the world. I have been informed by the British Legion that a relative of mine (unknown to me) James Ernest Beazley died on this day.

Southern Rhodesia became Rhodesia thereby severing its ties with Britain. Northern Rhodesia became Zambia and Nyasaland became Malawi. In the mid-seventies Rhodesia became Zimbabwe-Rhodesia, mainly to appease the world. The white minority government was on the point of financial collapse and in April 1980 elections were held. Robert Mugabe, head of a political party called ZANU, became premier. I personally never saw this coming as I thought Joshua Nkomo, who controlled the other prominent opposition party (ZAPU), would rise to the fore. He had been the main antagonist on behalf of the oppressed majority for many years dating back to the early sixties.

Mugabe dropped the Rhodesia part of the country's name and ever since it has been known as simply Zimbabwe. Mugabe is still its ruler. In 1983, he ensured his dominance by declaring ZAPU a banned organisation and confiscated Nkomo's numerous business interests. I was in fact appointed liquidator of Nkomo's assets, something I will go into more detail later.

Once the dust had settled, Mugabe made peace with Nkomo and instated him as one of two Vice Presidents. The other V.P was one of Mugabe's faithfuls, named Muzenda. Both these appointments were window dressing and it has always been Mugabe who kept complete control.

I find it incredible that Mugabe has maintained his position for more than thirty six years. It has to be one of the reasons that Zimbabwe has seen minimal internal conflict unlike so many other African states. I expect the troubles will start when Mugabe hands over power or dies of an old age. Indeed, there have been numerous protests in recent weeks. I have always been of the opinion that he has not relinquished his control as he could face a charge of crimes against humanity in The Hague. His massacre of the Matabele in 1983 must rank high as a punishable crime.

Take away the politics, Rhodesia, or Zimbabwe, whatever you want to call it, was for me the most wonderful place to work, raise a family and enjoy life on a grand scale. In the early days, it was regarded as the breadbasket of Africa. When I arrived, I found such a difference in attitude and friendliness of the African population compared to the indigenous people of South

Africa. I can't say I always understood their attitude to wealth; it simply was not that important. My first glimpse of this was on a pilot scheme on the Sabi River. Africans were given a piece of land on which to grow crops for their own benefit. All the inputs were supplied and assistance given once the crops were harvested. On average, £300 surplus was normal per piece of land. In 1957 this was a considerable sum. Do not think that the money would be used to make another similar sum the next harvest. No! The money was taken back to the villages and spent on African beer and riotous living. (This strikes me as the same philosophy my stepfather and his brothers had!)

Once the coffers were empty, the man would return to the Sabi in the hope of getting another piece of land on which to grow other crops. Of course, this hardly ever came to pass, as viable land is a scarce commodity and the demand outweighed the supply.

Working as a field geologist during those early years, I came across such an abundance of wildlife that most people would give their eye teeth to see. I recall walking through the bush in single file with my team of helpers, while thirty yards away passed a single file of eight giraffes going in the other direction, as though this was an everyday occurrence. A magical moment which ranks high on my list of unforgettable moments.

With this same team, I was taking samples of the river sands going up stream. I came to a small waterfall and stripped to cool my body in the trickle of water. While at it, one of my helpers grabbed my arm and yanked me aside, all the time pointing to a pride of lions having a feast on a recent kill, barely a stone's throw away. In my tired state, I had not even noticed them. Fortunately for me, the lions must have been well fed by then and took little interest in me and my helpers.

I had many other encounters with the wildlife, too many to detail. Out of it all, though, I learnt to respect their place on our planet.

1
Through The Years

I have managed to trace my ancestry back to a certain James Beazley who was born in Chester on the 4th March 1819, (recorded in Her Majesty's College of Arms). James Beazley became a prominent merchant ship owner and owned several tea clippers through his company Beazley & Co. The history of these amazing ships has been recorded in a book 'THE TEA CLIPPERS' by David MacGregor first published in 1952. Perhaps the most famous of his ships was the Robin Hood and just perhaps, that is why I am named Robin along with four other Christian names being Arthur Ernest Henry Nicholas. Robin was not included on my birth certificate which has caused me endless problems over the years. Nonetheless I have been called Robin from my earliest living memory.

Coincidentally, my third son Simon James was born on the 4th March 1987. The inclusion of the name 'James' was entirely accidental. The original James Beazley died in 1891.

James' eldest son, James Henry Beazley, was born in Birkenhead in September 1847 and his eldest son was Ernest Henry Beazley; (1876); my grandfather. Ernest Beazley was also a shipping man through his involvement with the first steam ship to sail between Liverpool and Canada. His exploits have also been recorded in a book entitled 'Whistle up the Inlet' and is the history of the Union Steamship Line. My father, Phillip Henry

Graham Beazley, was born in Canada in 1912. He married my mother Regina Zigadi on 2nd January 1937 in Athens.

I was born on 23rd November 1937; Canadian father, Greek mother. I have a sister who was born in 1939 and we lived in war zone Athens. For the most part I do not think this fact had any lasting affect on my life. One of my earliest recollections was going into the bomb shelters in the middle of the night and looking up at the search lights as they hunted the skies for enemy aircraft. I do not recall being scared or afraid, just interested.

My father had enlisted in the RAF (1935-1943) and on a trip to South Africa, decided it was the place in which he wished to settle his family. We sailed to Durban on the Athlone Castle in 1941 and, in due course, settled in at the Orange Grove Hotel in Johannesburg. My father returned to war duties with the British Army Middle East (1943-1946) and my mother took up a position in Pretoria translating for the government as she was proficient in six different languages.

My sister and I lived in a small house in the care of a German nanny near the city centre of Johannesburg. She could not speak Greek and we could not speak German. We settled on English as the common ground for communicating. She must have had excellent tutorial skills as by the time I was sent to boarding school I found I was far ahead of the rest of my class in both reading and arithmetic. Regrettably, I lost nearly all my Greek. Even to this day, while my understanding of the spoken language is fair, my communication skills are pretty thin. Such a shame.

I attended Parktown Preparatory School for boys as a boarder. I was five and a half years old. In 1951 I entered high school at Hilton College in Natal and matriculated in 1954. On leaving school I joined Anglo American Corporation as a trainee geologist at one of their gold mines on the East Rand. Two years later, my family moved to Southern Rhodesia and I was fortunate to be offered a job in Anglo's geological department in the field in Rhodesia. A three day duration train trip landed me at Salisbury railway station on the 7th April 1957. I little realised that I would remain there for the next 43 years.

After a few years in the African bush, I decided that I did not want to spend the rest of my days in the field and studied accountancy in which I qualified in 1965. I married a school teacher by the name of Valerie in 1961 and we settled in Salisbury. I left Anglo in 1962 and took up an office position with African Explosives and Chemical Industries Ltd. as a debtors' clerk which enabled me to make rapid progress with my studies. Valerie gave birth to our eldest son, Grayham, towards the end of 1962, a daughter, Penelope, in 1964 and a second son, Nicholas, in 1970.

I made good progress in my job at AE&CI and worked in its financial division. My boss was unqualified and as I could not see myself progressing past him, I resigned and joined a South African mining house as its Chief Agent in 1969. This company had embarked on geological investigations in Rhodesia and I feel I was tailor-made for the job. After a few years, with the changes to the political climate, the company had to curtail its activities in Rhodesia and on the first day of December 1973, I joined a group of companies called Supreme Holdings (Pvt.) Ltd., as the group accountant. On the second of January 1974, I informed George Palmer, the sole owner of Supreme, that the group was hopelessly insolvent. Shortly thereafter the group was placed into liquidation and George's estate was declared insolvent. At the time I went for my job interview with George, I could not have been more impressed. His office was decorated in the most up to date manner: thick pile carpeting; expensive furniture; silver pieces here and there. Several good paintings adorned the walls and, generally, I had the impression of lots of money. His car was a top of the range model as were the cars of the managers of his fourteen companies.

His business operations included several in the motor industry, a commercial radio and television station, an advertising and display company, as well as two funeral parlours. There was one major hiccup; all, and I mean all, his assets were on hire purchase through the several financial institutions operating in the country. His bank accounts were very much in the red. I have to mention that George's principal bank manager took his own life shortly after the full extent of the financial position of the group had been ascertained. There can be little doubt as to why.

At that first Christmas party, a member of staff passed out. Being an outsider due to my short involvement in the group, I don't recall the circumstances. I do however have a lasting memory of the man heading the funeral parlours, leaning over the prone figure with his hands in a moment of prayer. I think he was anticipating his next funeral case. When the companies were liquidated, this same man tried to appropriate the coffin lowering device for his personal use. The liquidator found out and summoned the man to his office. I have another lasting memory of the man in tears, crawling on his knees for some twenty yards pleading for forgiveness.

A liquidator named Woods was appointed; a man whom I grew to regard as having the utmost integrity and honesty and who I believe has shaped my own principles and ethics. The size of the group made this a considerable undertaking for any liquidator. As Woods was virtually a one man business, he asked me to assist him in winding up the group. I had not had much involvement with its financial state, but had acquired some knowledge of the group's activities during my month's long engagement with it. This seemed an ideal opportunity to broaden my financial skills and I agreed to join him on a temporary basis.

Woods was a large person and it was quite incongruous to see him riding around town on a tiny Vespa scooter. He nearly always wore a Safari suit and I think the only occasions he dressed more formally were to attend insolvency meetings in the High Court. He had served in India during the war years and I was regularly invited to 'pop out for a quick bite' at lunch time for a curry meal. He liked it 'hot'; I mean, really hot. I recall my eyes watering, going into an uncontrollable sneezing bouts and drinking gallons of cold water. I soon found myself making excuses not to join him for lunch and to this day avoid Indian cuisine if possible.

He commanded the highest degree of respect from all quarters. His business dealings were honest and straight forward. No nonsense anywhere.

In 1976, Rhodesia was experiencing grave economic difficulties. The value of its currency had declined dramatically. Exchange control was very tight. The banks permitted persons going out of the country on holiday a meagre allowance of Z$250 each. Woods went to England and shortly before his return he bumped into a friend and offered him what little foreign currency he no longer needed. When the friend returned to Rhodesia he paid the equivalent of what he had received in local currency into Wood's bank account.

Early one morning a police officer named Dave called in at the office to see Woods. I happened to know Dave having played squash against him in club matches on numerous occasions. I asked if I could help him but said he would call again a little later. He asked me to let Woods know he would be calling. When Woods came in, I told him Dave had been and would return shortly. Woods said he had to dash out briefly and would be back.

Dave returned and waited for some time for Woods but eventually left saying he would return the next day. The following day Woods failed to appear at the offices. On the following morning, we received the shattering news that Woods had taken his own life on a remote hill just outside of town. In due course, we learned that Woods had understood that Dave was conducting investigations on behalf of the Reserve Bank. This arose from the deposit made by his friend into Wood's bank account. He felt that this innocent transaction would bring shame on him, his family and his business.

What a waste! Why, oh why, had he not talked to someone; anyone? All for a few miserable dollars!

Following Woods' untimely death, his widow requested that I and another senior member of staff continue operating the business. It did not take long before we were able to buy out Mrs. Woods' share in the business and shortly thereafter my colleague left the country to settle in England. I acquired her shares in the trust company thereby becoming sole shareholder.

And so started the commencement of the rest of my working years until I officially retired on the millennium; 31st December 1999. I did unofficially spend a little more time tying up loose ends. These twenty-six years changed the course of my life and though they were not trouble free, I encountered fascinating events and experiences which have prompted me to write this biography. Through these years I have been divorced twice, remarried, grieved at the death of my third wife, and remarried again. I have sired five children; two sons and a daughter with my first wife and two more sons with my late wife, Brenda. I have a step daughter through my present wife, Wendy. I was briefly married to Alison after Valerie and will go into greater details of my marriages and their outcomes later. African tradition entitles me to a chief's status, as I have four sons.

I am retired and spend my days more or less doing what I want to. This is entirely due to the efforts of Wendy who works long hours, in order to maintain our present lifestyle. I do realise that I cannot play golf everyday due to the physical effort required. So, I play the piano (badly); paint (better than my piano playing) and keep my mind active with bridge, jigsaws puzzles and reading.

I only started painting when I was 70. I cannot emphasise how much pleasure I get out of it. I recommend to everyone that they give it a try. They could be surprised by what they achieve. I promise them hours and hours of pleasure and fun. I hear so many people saying "Oh. I couldn't possibly do that." Rubbish! Give it a bash!

I am the chief cook and bottle washer, and, also, do the regular shop for provisions. I enjoy cooking and try to surprise my family with unusual dishes. No comment! Now this epistle. I am not sure at this stage that it will ever be completed, let alone, printed, but I shall try to do so.

2

Parents

My father, Phillip Henry Graham Beazley, was born in Canada in 1912. He attended Shrewsbury School in England, a school where many of my ancestors were educated. I visited the school on one occasion when my sister enquired about enrolling her son. I have to admit at being overwhelmed at the reception Melody and I received. It felt like being on a royal visit. The school gave us a 'red carpet' welcome. Apart from a tour highlighting many of the achievements of our ancestors, we were also shown a record of the many achievements by the Beazleys. Most of my relatives excelled academically and in sport. My father's record was confined to the period of attendance; nothing more.

Phillip joined the RAF and was stationed in Athens where he met and married my mother, Regina Zigadi. Gina's father was a Pashta on the Greek island of Leros; something equivalent to a mayor, I believe. I have little other knowledge of my mother's family. During the war my father was sent to South Africa on a training exercise and then came back to Greece.

He decided South Africa was the best place for his family and we left Europe for Africa in 1941.

He returned to South Africa some months after the end of the war but could not settle down. His main activity centred round playing golf and gambling. He played exhibition golf with Bobby Locke, a household name in the sport. I remember being dragged along for eighteen holes fetching balls from under bushes. One such bush was occupied by a puff adder. No harm done but my visits to golf courses were curtailed there and then. I suspect my father collected a flea in his ear from my mother when she heard the story. This episode resulted in my avoiding the game of golf like the plague. Before long my mother, Gina, gave my father his marching orders. It did not take him long to find Mary, a very rich lady from Canada.

Although our family could not be placed in the wealthy league, I have never had a feeling of being deprived. I never received any form of pocket money and yet I never wanted for anything. Don't get me wrong; I am not a spoilt brat. It was just knowing that I never had to plead for anything from my parents.

My sister, Melody, and I were invited to spend a week at Mary's home in Houghton during a school holiday in 1947. Mary did not cook. She introduced me to tomato ketchup, a luxury I had not previously added to any meal, mainly because of being at boarding school. At home, steak and salad seemed to be the regular diet.

On the fourth night of our visit we had a very tasty cottage pie for supper. I made the huge mistake of asking for the ketchup not realising it was cook's night off and that Mary had prepared the meal. Mary went ballistic and ordered Phillip to "Get these bloody children out of here!" We went home to Gina early the next morning and I never saw my father again. He and Mary left Johannesburg and went to live in Vancouver shortly after.

That marriage did not last; I guess Mary realised that Phillip would never be a provider. She was good enough to place him in a sanatorium when his health deteriorated. He was diagnosed with having tuberculosis. The operation left him with only one half of a lung. Mary divorced him but did meet all his medical expenses. When he recovered, he married a nursing sister who had treated him at the sanatorium and they remained together for the rest of his life.

We did have contact many years later (1966) when he learned through my sister, now living in Greece, that he had two grandchildren living in Salisbury, Rhodesia. Shortly before Christmas we received an enormous box from Phillip which contained amazing presents for all of us. There was one snag; the customs duty on the presents was greater than my monthly salary!

Included with other presents was a tape recorder for which we were instructed to send messages to Canada. This task proved very difficult given the time span since our last communication. The children managed a few words of thanks as did Valerie and I. This method of contact died a very quick death from both sides.

I did hear from him once more in 1985. At that time I was in the process of leaving my second wife, Alison. Phillip had been told by my sister who had regular phone calls with him, that I was about to leave Alison. I picked up the phone when it rang and was told to "Stop being such a silly arse". End of call.

As already mentioned, Phillip remarried and lived in Calgary to the age of 86, this was quite remarkable having the use of only half of a lung. He spent his last few years teaching golf and bridge. My mother introduced me to the bridge table resulting in bridge remaining one of my passions in which I achieve moderate success from time to time.

My mother, Gina, now had another man in her life; George was a Greek. He adored my mother and was always good to her. As mentioned earlier, he had three other brothers and they were civil engineers mainly constructing dams and office blocks all over South Africa. George was a gentleman in every sense of the word. In due course, they married. He footed the bill for my sister's and my education at excellent high schools for which I am eternally grateful. However, a father he was not. Our relationship was one of quiet tolerance on both sides.

George's youngest brother was an architect; his oldest brother was the black sheep of the family and acted as the foreman on the various construction jobs they undertook. And the other brother was George's identical twin. They did everything together. It might be a picnic; it might be a holiday; it might be a dinner party. It did not matter; they did everything together.

Costas, the twin brother, was married and had a daughter, some ten years younger than me. One New Year's Eve (I think it was in 1955) the brothers followed Greek tradition, having a dinner party to see in the New Year. The early part of the evening was always devoted to gambling in the form of 'chemin de fer'. Now George and Costas used to share their good fortunes as well as their bad breaks. George was having a good run and was up a substantial amount when Costas arrived some two hours later. He demanded half of George's winnings. George felt that Costas was only entitled to join in from the time he arrived and would not give up any of his winnings.

I am not here to make a judgement call on the rights and wrongs of this decision. Suffice to say, Costas took exception and the two twins did not speak to each other for over six years.

Shortly after, the families moved to live in Greece. The wives did their utmost to break the deadlock and it was only when Costas was on his deathbed that George relented and went to make his peace. Costas died a few days later and now George, the twin, was convinced that his time on earth was up. He set about putting his affairs in order much to the bewilderment of my mother. He converted all their assets into cash and then prepared himself for death. His money was placed in several different accounts, mainly to avoid death duties, thus ensuring my mother was taken care of when he died. His daily routine consisted of washing, eating and drinking significant quantities of cheap Greek wine. He spent most of his waking hours watching the television morning, noon and night. Because he was now leading such a sedentary life, he did not die.

The weeks became months and the months became years. My sister had moved to Athens with George and Gina and was gainfully employed. Some eleven years after Costas' death, Melody came home from work one evening and found George dead in front of the television. He had choked to death on a peanut! The irony of this sudden death was that most of the money he had squirrelled away was never found. To this day it is lying in some banks; that is if the Greek government has not appropriated the funds.

Several years later, my mother, like my father, died at the age of 86. In all my years I had never seen Gina with a hair out of place. Her skin was always wrinkle free. She must have spent a fortune on skin creams and hairdressers. When my sister thought our mother's days were drawing to a close, she called me to visit my mother, probably for the last time. When I entered her bedroom I got the shock of my life to see this grey haired woman who was my mother. But even more of a shock was seeing her hands and face which were still as smooth as silk. Really spooky! She greeted me asking, "What are you doing here?" She died two weeks later.

Am I, too, destined to live to the age of 86? Some days I feel I could live for ever; others, a few months at best. Not that I am complaining. I count myself as one of the lucky ones and any ailments I have are only of a minor nature. Nevertheless, if one experiences a severe headache, for example, one can be forgiven for fearing the end is nigh. One thing I am certain of and that is that I shall not spend my days in front of the television waiting for the end. Hopefully my end will come swiftly. I cannot bear the thought of living to an age where I could not manage to care for myself.

In recent years I joined an organisation which cares for the aged. My function was visiting old men who were on their own and spending a few hours a week in their company. The one common thing I became acutely aware of was the smell of urine permeating their homes. I really don't want that for me.

My trust company acted as secretaries for a wealthy retired auctioneer. Frank lost his wife of many years, shortly before retiring. He married the widow of an acquaintance of ours shortly after. Within a month of the marriage Frank had a stroke. He was completely immobilized and spent all his waking hours in a wheelchair. His poor newlywed wife had to care for his personal needs which she did tirelessly and without complaint or any help. It took six long years before Frank passed away. Her thanks for her devotion to duty was verbal assault and abuse from Frank's offspring. They accused her of stealing his money, neglecting him and, worst of all, having an affair. As his company secretary, I knew his funds were intact and I knew his wife was not the sort of person they made her out to be. In the end, she walked away empty-handed.

3

Schools

In 1942, at the tender age of five and a half, I entered Parktown Preparatory School for boys. As there had been an outbreak of one of the common childhood diseases I was not permitted to start at the commencement of the term. My appearance thoroughly displeased my class teacher as this would disrupt her tuition. She requested me to recite the alphabet. I mentioned earlier that our 'nanny' had taught me many things and so I was able to rattle off my ABC. Mrs Pargiter, the teacher, said that I was wrong. So, I repeated the alphabet again but more slowly in case I had left out a letter on my first attempt. Again, I was informed that I was incorrect. I should have said "Ah, for apple, Baa, for bat, ca, for cat," etc. etc. What a way to start school!!

    I did get over that initial hiccup and made good progress through the years being one of the top three scholars by the time I was ready for high school. Outside the classroom however, life was more difficult. The dormitories were situated above the headmaster's quarters. Our beds consisted of a coir mattress on a chainlike frame. The slightest movement in bed brought the headmaster roaring upstairs demanding we kept perfectly still. Some years later it occurred to me that he probably thought we were playing with ourselves! To this day I am still a very restless sleeper and must alter my sleeping position over a hundred times in a night. You can imagine what agony I went through in those early days.

Perhaps even more traumatic was the fact that I was bigger in stature than my contemporaries. This resulted in my being the target for the bullies. Like many tall beings I was never the aggressive type. This fact did not help me. Even in the organised sports I was frequently singled out and, more often than not, when it came to boxing. I hated it. I had to face up to the school boxing champion. Week after week I got thumped, trying my utmost to put on a brave face. Finally, sometime around the latter years of prep school, I decided enough was enough. Once more I had to face the school boxing champ, a lad named Price. I still remember his name and what he looked like. At the clang of the bell I leapt out of my corner and literally smashed him. I was informed later that I was shouting like an enraged bull as I hit him and hit him until I was physically pulled off while the blood poured from his eyes, nose and mouth. From that day on I never suffered any form of bullying again.

I have one other lasting memory from my prep school days and that had to do with boarding school food. Generally, it was pretty awful. But, I must remember that it was during the war and the years that followed, I particularly hated pumpkin and marrow. Lunch was the main meal of the day. For many years, I was matron's pet and usually sat beside her on a bench near the top of the table. Matron sat in a chair at the top. On this particular day, I was not feeling well and low and behold we were served both pumpkin and marrow. I wanted to throw up at the thought. In desperation, I distracted Matron's attention by pointing out something supposedly going on behind her. When she turned her head, I slid the pumpkin and marrow off my plate onto the floor. Matron's face turned a bright red as she swung her gaze around to me. The pumpkin and marrow had landed on her foot. I think she believed I had soiled my pants. When she saw what I had done, she grabbed me by my ear and frogmarched me to the headmaster's study where I received six of the best. I was told to think of all the starving children in the world who would give their eye teeth for my pumpkin and marrow. In my opinion, they were welcome to it.

In truth, I was very fond of Mrs. Spring, our matron. She was a surrogate mother to us boarders and was always kind and understanding of our needs.

I know now that I found my independence in those years which I believe has helped me so much in my later life. I rarely saw my mother, no criticism intended. That's the way it was. My sister was also placed in boarding school at Roedean. Both prep schools attended Sunday school at the Anglican Church near the schools and I nearly always caught a glimpse of her in the crocodile march after the service. We did get together for the Christmas holidays but for most of the years our respective terms overlapped, as one school was a three term a year school and the other a four term school. I cannot remember which was which.

We did have one school holiday together in 1949. We went to Mozambique and stayed at the Polana Hotel in Lorenzo Marques (now Maputo). The hotel belonged to the Schlesingers, a very wealthy family from South Africa with vast holdings in hotels and cinemas. Peter Schlesinger, the only son of Susan, was also on holiday at the time and was my age. We became firm friends and spent many times together. I was aware of the difference in our families' financial status but it did not seem to matter.

At some point in the year I was staying with Peter when his aunt, Ann, returned from the U.S.A. We all went to meet her in her suite at the Carlton Hotel (very posh!) I was immediately dazzled by her beauty and 'niceness'. At some point during the evening Ann noticed her purse containing all her jewellery was missing. The police were called in and Peter and I joined the search; all very exciting. I was looking outside on a balcony and though it was pretty dark, noticed some object about two floors below. I told the police and, sure enough, they discovered it was the missing purse. Ann gave me a huge kiss as reward. I fell in love instantly.

An interrogation of the hotel staff who had serviced the suite during the evening eventually produced the culprit.

That Christmas holiday, I was Peter's guest at the Polana Hotel. Ann was also there; I was a happy little boy. I do remember getting sick, probably too much sun. I also remember that Ann was the most sympathetic. On such things, little boy's daydreams are made. I remember wishing she was my mother.

At the end of the holidays Peter and I went to our respective new high schools. I went to Hilton and Peter went to Michaelhouse. As the two schools are bitter rivals, Peter and I, sadly, grew apart and within a year lost all contact.

I felt indeed privileged to be attending Hilton College, one of South Africa's top educational facilities for boys. The number of scholars approximated 350. I am not sure if this is still the case as I heard that the sixth form had been opened to girls. Hilton is set in the countryside in Natal, well off the main road to Pietermartzburg. New boys were boarded in Falcon House for their first year and thereafter allocated to one of the other five houses. There are no day scholars. One of the standing rules for new boys was that they would not be caned during the first month. Having come from prep school where I was only caned on four occasions during my eight years there, I did not anticipate any problems. How wrong can a big headed young person be? During homework in the first week the fellow next to me had drawn a figure of an African chief with a huge 'John Thomas'. He passed it to me just as a prefect walked behind me and saw the drawing in my hand. I was taken to the prefects' study and given four of the best with a long cane. A little harsh I would say. Incidentally the artist had written the name of

'ZOG' on the drawing and from that day on till I left school my nickname was ZOG.

I shall not go into full details but have to report that during that first term I was caned eight times, more than my entire prep school period and considerably more the remaining four years at Hilton. There is one other caning occasion worth relating which happened during my third year.

For some time the food in the main dining hall had been pretty awful. On the morning of this particular episode the word went out by a group, I shall call the ringleaders, for want of a better collective name, that all boys, except for Falcon House who had meals in a separate dining hall, would stage a protest strike that night. As luck would have it the food dished up was even worse than ever. I can recall the dessert was particularly horrible; an indigestible square of stodgy fruit pie and burnt custard. Someone in the hall started hissing, a sound that was taken up by us all very quickly. The prefect on duty that night told us to stop immediately at which point, one of the ringleaders stood up and shouted "To the gates." These were on the boundary of the school grounds and nearly a mile away from the main building. Three hundred or so boys went marching to the gates singing merrily. On arrival at the gates the ringleaders called a halt to the march and while we all gathered round they debated on our next move. It was now for the first time I witnessed the power of the 'mob'. I am sure the ringleaders expected us to return to our dormitories as the demonstration must have had some effect on the administration.

We were having none of it and the mob, which we now were, took over and continued our march to the main road some four miles away. The atmosphere was electric. And jubilant. Every so often, as we marched singing down the road, we saw the lights of a motor car coming from school looking for us. I still can't believe how quickly three hundred people could disappear from view; not once but at least half a dozen times as the cars searching for us travelled backwards and forwards. We finally arrived at the highway and assembled in a forest by the side of the road where we could keep a lookout. Nobody slept that night. Some enterprising boys raided a nearby chicken farm and returned with several chickens including, I fear, some very large prize cockerels. A number of large fires had been started as it was bitterly cold being the middle of winter (rather dangerous as we were after all in a forest). The chickens were 'cooked' and most people had a taste.

I guess the end to our protest was predictable. One of the ringleaders went back to school and returned to the forest with several housemasters. We were told that we should return to our respective dormitories with the undertaking that the incident and other grievances would be thoroughly investigated. That night we were all caned 'six of the best'. By the time I received my six, our housemaster was so exhausted that the caning was more symbolical than painful. Nevertheless, the outcome was very gratifying; the headmaster was fired and there was a dramatic improvement in our meals.

My scholastic record has few highlights. In fact I hardly did anything of note. I tried art; not good! I then tried my hand at carpentry. I made two items. The first was a ping pong table. Regrettably I did not check the measurements. Diagonally, there was a difference of twelve inches in the two measurements. My next and last effort was a tray on which I intended to serve my mother breakfast in bed. I say it myself, it really was well made; big and strong. The disappointment came when I could not get the laden tray through the bedroom door; length and width were too big!

In Africa the rains fall in the summer months, usually November to March. The Hilton estate is bounded to the north by the Umgeni River which is in flood in January. All boys have to vacate the immediate school area on Sundays, and take a 'picnic' lunch to any part of the estate they wish. Naturally the flooding Umgeni is a huge attraction. One is able to jump into a large pool and get swept down the river for about a mile to a large rock. Here one seeks dry land and then proceeds back up stream to the big pool for the next trip down. It really is fantastic fun; unless you are not a swimmer.

At the start of one year such a boy in his first week came to the river with his friends and witnessed them having the time of their lives. So much so that without thinking he got caught up in the moment and plunged into the river. Being a non-swimmer he had no control on his direction and was carried by the current to the far side of the river. When he reached the big rock, witnesses saw him being carried away. Many boys tried to catch up with him by running further down the river. All to no avail. By 4.00p.m. all boys had to return to their dormitories to get dressed in their school uniforms for Even Song held in the school chapel at 6.00.p.m.

The incident had been reported to the housemaster where the boy slept. I expect a search party had been organised.

In the chapel; in a moment of prayer and in absolute silence we all heard the pitter-patter of little feet. There, unbelievably, was the lad walking to his allotted seat. We learnt later that an African on the far side of the river had seen the boy, jumped in, grabbed him and swam and deposited him safely on the school side of the river. Quite remarkable!

I matriculated at the end of 1954. That year I was made a school prefect (as opposed to a house prefect) and, I believe, learnt how to exercise the correct amount of authority without being overzealous. I achieved some degree of success academically and in sport. I even learnt to dance and attended inter-school dances as a blind date. I even found a quick solution to boxing classes.

Another lad and I were facing off and one of us incurred a bloody nose. The gym master, concerned for blood on his gym floor, sent both of us to the showers with a pat on the back for 'excellent work'. You can guess what followed. From then on, we took turns in getting a nose bleed in the shortest possible time. Sure enough; we were hastily dispatched to the showers to 'recover'.

Overall it was a very good year for me.

4

Falling In Love

My philosophy on love is quite simple. I do not believe there is only one person for us to live and love forevermore on this planet. I liken choosing a partner to writing exams. You can achieve 100% in exams on several different subjects. Likewise you can find perfection in several different persons. More often than not, your degree of perfection may not reach 100%. Only you can decide when your endeavours have achieved a point where you find satisfaction. Regrettably, like exams, we sometimes fail in both our exams and our relationships.

Having spent my entire schooling years in a boy's only environment, I have to admit to being extremely awkward around girls. Don't get me wrong. I simply love the opposite sex. I fall in and out of love like a yo-yo. I suppose we all have different definitions of what constitutes true love. For myself, what I see in a face is the cornerstone of any connection. We all know beauty is in the eye of the beholder. Even though beauty is only skin deep, I start with the face, then the laugh, next the voice and, following closely behind, is the personality. Intelligence is an essential ingredient as is emotion followed by sentiment. Lust, on the other hand, plays no part in my feelings of love. For me, big breasts are a turn-off. Love for a woman should embrace respect, a feeling of wanting to spend quality time together and understanding the other's point of view. Passion does come into it but is down the list and only comes when all the other ingredients are in place. (No doubt, a throwback to boarding school.)

Doris Day was the start of my day dreaming and at one stage I fell for a girl who looked a little like her. Our one and only date was at the cinema with a group of friends. She sat on the extreme left of the group; I sat on the extreme right. We had exchanged a couple of phone calls when she told me she had met a chap with a motorbike and asked what sort of motorbike I had. Hell; I didn't even own a bicycle. We never got as far as holding hands.

I now started imagining my life with dozens of girls, mostly film stars, and that's where it ended; in my imagination. I just did not know how to set about taking the first steps to make contact. I most certainly was never a charmer. I clearly remember, with considerable embarrassment, a lovely young lady whom I dated regularly but never got to kiss. I was just too scared. Poor Sally! Poor me! I also remember a pretty girl I met on a train. We agreed to meet at the zoo on the next Sunday. As luck would have it the heavens opened up on that day. She never pitched and I got soaked. I hadn't even thought to ask her for her phone number. Just how pathetic is that?

In my final year at Hilton, one of my very good friends, Geoff, had a girlfriend at St. Anne's. This girls' school is situated at Hilton Road, some five miles from Hilton College. Geoff persuaded me to accompany him on a visit to see his girlfriend on a Sunday afternoon. The enticement was that I would meet a very nice young lady while he was spending time with his friend. The problem of transport was solved when Geoff borrowed two bicycles from the kitchen staff.

Had we been caught it would have resulted in probable expulsion from school and as school prefects we were expected to set the example to all the other scholars. As luck would have it, the day was typical of the weather for that time of the year;

misty and drizzly. By the time we arrived at St. Anne's we were both soaked.

Jenny, my date, turned out to be a pretty girl and also proved to be a really nice, friendly person. I, naturally, immediately 'fell in love.' After tea, we had to return to our school. By now the heavens had really opened up, and we got soaked again within minutes. We encountered no problems probably due to prevailing weather conditions.

We even managed another couple of visits. Jenny had agreed to go out with me during the next school holidays and our first outing would be to an afternoon matinee. As I had no means of transport, Jenny said she would collect me. Imagine my surprise when this spanking new Rolls Royce arrived driven by a chauffeur with Jenny in the back seat. I had not realised that Jenny came from a very wealthy family.

And I suppose it was the difference in our family status that eventually ended our happy, innocent times together. Or, perhaps, Jenny tired of going out with someone who only showed affection by holding hands!

In 1955 I received military call up papers. I was enlisted as a gunner in the Transvaal Horse Artillery and was posted to Potchefstroom. My first week in camp was a huge cultural shock. Having had such a sheltered upbringing, I found the world also consisted of some very rough types. Luckily, I was put on an officers' training course. Even luckier still, I was billeted with a chap I had been to Hilton with. And the luckiest part of all, Colin was not shy of girls. Tagging along with him I met the first girl I think I actually fell in love with. Sandy was a stunner and qualified in all departments mention earlier but she did not want to have anything to do with chaps from the army.

In the winter of 1956, I visited Potchefstroom as a member of Eastern Transvaal's rugby team. After the game, I contacted Sandy telling her I was in town. She rallied some of her girlfriends and invited the younger members of the team to a party. I do not remember much of the evening as I only had eyes for this beautiful girl who had come back into my life. I cannot even begin to guess how many hours I subsequently spent thinking and daydreaming about her.

As I was no longer in army uniform she invited me to spend the following weekend with her and her family. A sort of 'get to know you' weekend. The weekend was great and the invitation was extended to other weekends.

When I left South Africa to reside in Rhodesia in April 1957 we had reached an understanding that we were an item, though not necessarily exclusive. I was still a virgin. In a letter, Sandy expressed feelings of frustration that I had not attempted to make more intimate contact. My excuse arose from being a guest in her parents' home. In reality, I was being a wimp.

Days before leaving for Rhodesia I 'fell in love' with Doreen. We exchanged many, many letters declaring undying love and how we were longing to see each other. When the moment arrived about a year later, it only took one look; there was nothing. This was a sure case of falling in love with love.

I lost my virginity to Elaine at the beginning of the next year, when I was 20 years of age. She was sexy. She was hot. I experienced feelings of lust that were new and unexpected but I doubt if love came into the equation. And she wanted to get married. Fortunately, I did not lose my head all together and was sensible enough to realise I was still young and immature. I, actually, broke off contact within a couple of weeks. I was stationed in the colliery town of Wankie at the time. I was one of a number of geologists from Anglo. We enjoyed a good social life after working hours. All the other men had dates while I was the odd one out. They persuaded me to start dating Elaine again and I must admit I did not need much persuasion. (This mainly arose due to the fact that, in between time, a certain pretty maid I had my eyes on was also making eyes at me. I found out she was married, only when her rather huge husband warned me to lay off! Scary!)

A year later I told Elaine that I was not ready for marriage for one thing. For another, I told her that I could not see her living in the field as a geologist's wife. Perhaps I was put off, even further, when I found a letter in her handbag from some poor young man whose emotions had more than likely been aroused as had mine. I told her she would always be remembered as my first lover.

An earlier remark from my mother regarding Elaine's suitability had no doubt done something to influence my decision. My mother was a terrible snob. I doubt she would have approved of any young lady in whom I showed an interest. Elaine tried the usual tricks to collar me, even to tell me she was expecting. Time proved her to be a liar! I did experience some sleepless nights in the interim.

Some years later my first wife was in the nursing home after the birth of our first child. When I paid a visit, I recognised the lady in the adjacent bed. She had been a very close friend of Elaine's. She told me how lucky I was as Elaine had married shortly after we had parted and her husband's life had been turned into a living hell.

I must mention another Jenny who came into my life. This happened at a time I was settled into a comfortable existence with my first wife and three young children. Jenny and Eric moved into the neighbourhood and threw an evening party to meet their new neighbours. The evening degenerated and after a couple of hours everyone was in the swimming pool laughing and shouting. No one was completely naked but I am sure all the men had their eyes on Jenny whose figure was quite stunning. Her bra and panties left little to the imagination. To add to the interest in her, she had a French family connection and frequently blushed coyly when paid a compliment, of which there were an unusual number.

I must confess that I found the evening uncomfortable and I suspect my wife also had her reservations. (Call me stuffy if you wish.) I did not see much of Jenny for some time; only at other parties. By then it had come to everyone's notice that Eric, her husband, was behaving like a tom cat. Some months later, Jenny joined the squash club of which I was Chairperson. I came to realise in fact, she was not the party girl type at all. Over time, we became very good friends; often played squash and tennis together; all completely platonic. (This was more than likely due to the fact that Ann had come into my life; also through the squash club.) I even took up an appointment as the liquidator of Eric's garage business and successfully sorted out their financial problems. Many years later, my present wife and our three younger children spent a very enjoyable weekend with Jenny and Eric when we went to Durban on one of my wife's business trips.

It was, therefore, with some considerable sadness I later learnt that Jenny had left Eric and taken up holy orders.

And I must not forget Sheila. What a beautiful girl! She could have graced the cover of any glossy fashion magazine. Unfortunately, she was married to Brian, a rough but very likeable rogue from Zambia who made her life hell. As we were virtually neighbours, Sheila frequently phoned my wife for help. I would rush to Sheila's home to ensure she and their two young children were ok as Brian took to a little physical force from time to time. More often than not, I found her in tears. Brian was a heavy drinker (along with other vices) and seemed hell bent on destroying his marriage. He also got himself involved with other shady types from Zambia. I bailed him out of gaol on more occasions than the fingers on my left hand. He frequently accused me of wanting to have an affair with his wife. We both laughed at the idea! More often than not, he would insist on having a pint as soon as he had been released on bail.

Sheila got her divorce; I got my divorce; but our destinies

went in different directions. She moved to Johannesburg and my family was always made welcome when we travelled through Jo'burg on holiday. We remain good friends.

5

Wives

Valerie

Fortunately, I think, for me, Mother and George left Rhodesia to return to Greece in 1959. At that time, I was stationed near a small mining town called Gwanda. A certain music teacher at the junior school in the village caught my eye. Enter Valerie. The teachers at the school invited all the young men to a social evening. I tried to date Val in the weeks that followed but she would have nothing to do with me. (I learnt later she was still pining over a young man she had met at university in Cape Town.) However, just as I was turning my attention in other directions, I was invited to tea.

And so began a friendly but certainly not romantic period during which we went to dinner, the cinema, sports events but never anything too close. About this time in Rhodesia's history a Joshua Nkomo was rousing his troops and causing disturbances all around the country. Val was transferred to another mining town, Mashaba. I did my duty and went visiting over weekends, again all platonic. As I had to drive back to Gwanda late at night, Val gave me some pills to keep me awake.

I have to admit, the pills didn't do a great job in stopping me from falling asleep at the wheel but over the weeks I found I lost a lot of weight; something I probably needed. Val had been giving me Tenuate, a weight loss pill which was subsequently banned.

During 1960, Val's mother became increasingly anxious about her little girl as the Nkomo situation had become considerably worse. Val decided it was time for us to get married and on the 7th of January 1961 I married the girl of my current dreams. My mother could not interfere but she did fly out for the occasion. We honeymooned in Durban where Val caught too much sun on the very first day. The local doctor saw more of her that week than I did.

We set up home in a flat in Avondale, Salisbury and during that year Val and I both went to work. Our daily routine included a morning bath together during which my music teaching wife instructed me on how to sing in key. She would tell me to sing "Laaa", which I did. Then she would repeat the process in several different keys. What a way to start each day!

I had decided that I did not wish to spend the rest of my days in the field and had already commenced studies to become an accountant. I managed to secure a desk job with African Explosives & Chemical Industries Ltd. Here, with my success in my studies I was promoted and felt reasonably satisfied with my life. During 1962 we moved from the flat into a small house with a garden. Val had left her dog, called Barney, with her mother and was now able to bring him to our house.

One very dark night while I was sound asleep, Val gripped my thigh and whispered that someone was climbing in through our bedroom window. I jumped out of bed cursing furiously. The intruder did a backflip and in the process twisted his ankle or something as I heard him cry out in pain. I dashed to the kitchen and released Barney who stormed out of the house running round and round and round. Nothing! The intruder had got away. I alerted the nearby police station and some fifteen minutes later an African constable arrived. Barney went ballistic and had the constable on the ground in seconds threatening to tear him to pieces. Very, very embarrassing.

Late in November 1962 Val gave birth to our first child, Grayham George Nicholas, as we later christened him. Just under two years later Penelope Edith was born and our little house was now too little. We rented a huge double story house in Avondale where we spent some five happy years. We were as poor as church mice as Val had obviously had to give up work to care for our children and we only had my salary on which to survive. Matters were made worse with the introduction of PAYE. I have already mentioned the shock of having to pay a huge amount of customs duty on the presents sent to us by my father. We bought our house as the monthly payment on the mortgage was less than the rent we had been paying out. This proved to be a fortuitous move as, a few years later, we were able to sell the house making a good profit, which was enough to put down on a plot in the area of Chisipite, We were able to afford to build a really nice bungalow designed by Val. Our third child, Nicholas, was born early in 1970.

I have mentioned we were poor. Our first holiday with our two elder children was a trip to Fishhoek in the Cape. Val's mum, Edith, and her second husband, Archie, lived in a small house near the beach. Edith was a cheerful person while Archie was quite the opposite. They kindly borrowed four beds for us which were placed in the garage. It did not matter; we were together and we were on holiday!

One day on the beach, I saw a bright object in the sand. It was a very expensive gent's watch. There was an inscription on the back but I can no longer remember it. I handed it in at the beach kiosk. A week later, I was buying some cool drinks and the kiosk manager handed the watch back to me stating no one had claimed it. I was delighted and discussed what to do with it. On our last but one day, Archie lent me his car to take Val and the kids for a drive. It was a very windy day; Cape South Easters are notorious. I tried to find a sheltered spot out of the wind and saw a low wall near the sea. I left the car to investigate whether we would find shelter behind the wall.

Unfortunately, I had not closed my door properly. The strength of the wind thrust the door open and I turned to see the car with my wife and children being blown along gathering speed as it approached the edge of the beach. I had terrifying visions of losing my family to the sea. Luckily, at the last second the wind snapped the door right back and the car stopped still. My relief was immense; until I saw the damage to the car door's hinges and side mirror.

We had no money left to have the car repaired. We solved the problem of what to do with the watch and gave it to Archie to compensate him for the damage to his car. All very embarrassing. We caught the train back to Rhodesia the next day.

A few weeks later, Archie took his car to the garage to have the door repaired. The manager noticed the watch on Archie's wrist and asked him where he had got it from. It transpired the watch belonged to the manager's father and had much sentimental value. He told Archie that his father's watch bore an inscription on the back and this confirmed that the watch did indeed belong to the claimant. Archie, reluctantly, parted with the watch; the good news though, he had his car repaired free of charge.

In 1970, Val gave birth to our third child, a son whom we named Nick. I recall visiting Val and our baby in the hospital with a black eye which I had sustained at work.

I qualified as an accountant in 1965 and early in 1969 left AE&CI to join another South African company as their Chief Agent. The money was better but not nearly enough to please my wife who accused me of lacking ambition. The black eye was inflicted on me by a drilling contractor who had taken exception to my shouting at his mother over the telephone. I do not deny shouting but I could not hear what she had to say and vice versa. When this driller came to the office at the close of the working day I explained the circumstances and asked him to phone his mother to ascertain what offensive words, if any, had upset her. He phoned her and, during their conversation, I had to point out that he too was now shouting at his mother over the phone to make himself understood. Apart from looking somewhat foolish, I could see he would only be satisfied with knocking my brains out. We agreed to do it outside rather than in the office. I was still surprised when he threw the first punch as he was a least a foot shorter and some 50 lbs less in weight. The result was predictable. I had opened a deep cut over one of his eyes and he could hardly see through all the blood. I confess to feeling sickened by its sight and decided to try to finish it quickly which I did with an almighty punch to his head. He dropped like a stone. I asked him if he had had enough as I had just injured my thumb on his head. He begrudgingly agreed. Just as well as I doubt I could have carried on due to the stabbing pains shooting through my thumb. When he got up, he offered me his hand with the words "no hard feelings?" He had to be kidding!!

My wife was not too impressed. I wondered if my new born son would have approved.

The political scene in Rhodesia deteriorated over the next few years. Ian Smith became Prime Minister and we were shunned by Britain. Nkomo's renegades got really active and we all found ourselves on military service. I was enrolled in Dads army which was used in a protective role. The indigenous population in the countryside was herded into villages which were fenced into 'keeps'. Our function was to prevent them supplying the insurgents with food and shelter and to stop the insurgents from finding safety in the keeps.

Army call-ups made work very difficult for me. My business of liquidating had surged with the collapse of so many companies finding it impossible to continue operating without breaking the insolvency laws. Apart from the liquidations my trust company had a healthy number of clients whose books we maintained and I also had an investment arm to the firm which multiplied in size as the rate of inflation increased. The number of employees in my company had more than doubled and it was imperative that they had a boss on hand to help with day-to-day problems. The army was quite understanding and eventually transferred me to the Paycorps. Here, I managed to cut my army duties from six week spells to shorter periods though they became more frequent to make up my full period of duty.

Before being transferred, I and thirty other men were sent to the Mozambique border. Our duty was to protect some workers who were cutting fire breaks along the supposed border between to the two countries. I cannot prove that what happened was deliberate or just bad luck. On one of our patrols, we were suddenly surrounded by huge fires. The flames must have been twenty feet high and the gusts of wind created by the fire draft were intense. The sky above us was black with smoke. The roar from the fire was deafening. It seemed there was no way out and that we risked being severely burnt or worse. It was only due to one of the local Africans working for us that we survived. He led us into an underground cavern that had been carved out over the centuries by an old river. This cavern, on a normal day, would have been like a fairy's paradise as it was unbelievably beautiful. We survived; all but one; one of our group was missing. A charred object was located the next day and we speculated that it was a body belonging to the person who had tried to burn us alive. Wishful thinking; my view is that he had ducked at the first opportunity and was probably back with other militants across the border.

I was transferred to the Paycorp. While preparing pay for those currently on call-up, I noticed that the group I had last been with had once again been despatched to the same area. I was therefore somewhat surprised to see a man from that group walking into the office. We had become good friends while on duty and played chess together when we had spare time. I extended my right hand in greeting and was shocked when he took my hand with his left hand. It was then I noticed his right arm was missing. He told me that the troop had come under heavy attack during which one soldier died and several were injured. It dawned on me that but for the transfer, I would have been with those men. Frightening thought.

Once Mugabe came into power in 1980, the army required one more duty of us before we were disbanded. That duty was to make a payment to the thousands of persons claiming to have assisted Mugabe in overthrowing Smith's government.

I was sent along with about fifty other pay office soldiers to a remote area in the South-east of Zimbabwe. Some thirty thousand people had assembled there to collect an amount of Z$350 each. If you do the arithmetic, you will see we were holding over Z$10,500000. A little scary to say the least. It did however demonstrate to us how strong a hold Mugabe had over his minions as we experienced no problems at all.

After satisfactorily proving their identity, each claimant, he, or she, as the case might be, were paid the Z$350. They were then permitted to put Z$10 in their pocket and the balance of Z$340 was placed in a trunk. The supervision of the payment was carried out by Mugabe's elite soldiers and not by any of us who had served in the army under Smith. Several of the recipients of pay tried to run off with their full amount, only to be thumped to the ground by the protecting soldiers. In these instances, the full Z$350 was retained and the offender sent off empty-handed. Despite the public nature of the beatings and the confiscation of all the money, the attempts to get away with all their Z$350, continued. The whole exercise took three days and I regret to say that I personally witnessed two persons shot dead and a third so badly beaten, I doubt he survived.

We were only one small section of the payment operations

being carried out all over Zimbabwe. I wonder what happened to the many millions of dollars retained by Mugabe's men.

However, the problems on the political scene did not end with a cash settlement. Bands of aggrieved persons maintained a constant stream of raids on white farmers throughout the country. It is with much sadness I record the murder of Val's sister, her husband, his mother, his brother and one of their daughters. This happened at Christmas time 1980 on their farm in the Kezi district; so much for peace and goodwill to all mankind.

I fear I have strayed from the topic of my wives so will now return to the thread. After returning from a military stint towards the end of 1977, Val informed me that her psychologist wanted to see me. I didn't know she even had one! I duly made an appointment and was distressed to learn I had a very unhappy wife. I know our sex life was almost non-existent but, that apart, I was under the illusion that the rest of our marriage was pretty much ok. Valerie had hired an architect who designed and constructed a fantastic extension to our home; the children were all growing up and doing well in school. There was even a little money in the bank.

The last thing I wanted was to have an unhappy wife. We discussed a divorce but agreed to have a holiday at Christmas time to explore any possibility of saving the marriage. A holiday was booked at Wavecrest, a seaside resort in the Transkei. This is a fairly remote and underdeveloped area of South Africa and the last twenty miles to the hotel was the worst stretch of road I have ever encountered, taking well over two hours to complete. It did not auger well for our future relationship and so it proved. At the end of our stay we agreed that we would part as soon as we could. I think I should say that at no time were there more than a few angry exchanges; mostly indifference. We had lasted seventeen years together. Our divorce papers are dated 22nd March 1978. (By some strange quirk of fate, my third wife's birthday happened to be the 22nd of March. Is that weird or is that weird?)

I can't say that I did not wish for a more active partner when it came to the sex side of our relationship.

I, also, can say that apart from a kiss and a cuddle with a girl in the office, I managed to keep my marriage vows intact.

The holiday was not a complete washout as I caught the two largest fish of my life, both well over 15lbs. The last was just before we left the resort and we were able to take it back to Rhodesia. (More on this later.) Soon after returning to our home I was fortunate in finding lodgings in a large beautifully appointed home belonging to Mrs. Joy Yeatman. Val even came with me to ensure the lodging was suitable for her soon to be ex-husband. Joy was a wonderful old sole and once I had survived a thorough interview from her son George (from London) I was accepted and treated like one of the family.

I am not quite finished with Val yet. Three months after finalising our divorce she married a wealthy Canadian man named Mike Yates. (Don't get confused with my landlady.) What happened next was one of the most bizarre occurrences I have experienced. On the eve of their departure on honeymoon to Canada, Val asked me to look after her jewellery box. I was given to understand that it contained, among other items, the diamond engagement ring, an emerald eternity ring and one other valuable piece I had given her during our years together. I decided the safest place for them would be in my vault at the office. I locked the box in the glove compartment of my car for the night. Next morning, I drove into town and parked in the city's large multi-storey carpark. I did not have a permanent space and found a random parking space on the fourth floor.

At morning tea time, I suddenly remembered the jewellery box in my car in the car park. I hurried to the fourth floor and, horror of horrors, I found my car with all four doors open. I felt absolutely sick as I opened the glove box. This was followed instantly, by the utmost relief, when I saw the jewellery box was still there. I opened the box and found many expensive pieces along with a couple of gold Kruger Rand and another few gold lozenges. But not any of the valuable pieces I had given Val!

I called the police and they promptly took fingerprints etc. including mine. Over many months, the parking garage had experienced numerous car break-ins, almost on a daily basis. On this particular day, there was only one. My car! Here is the dilemma. Why had the thief taken only the valuable items I had given Val? Why had the thieves not taken the whole box? Why had they not taken the Kruger Rand and gold lozenges which were all easily negotiable items? Why was my car, parked on the fourth floor, the only one broken into? It is just possible that the thieves did not notice the jewellery box and the valuable pieces were never in it, in the first place. But I cannot escape the fact that my car, and only my car, had been broken into.

I received confirmation that Val and Mike were already in Canada and had to tell Val what happened. She confirmed that the box did contain the missing items. There was no insurance to cover the loss.

To this day I still lose sleep trying to fathom the puzzle.

Val and Mike returned from their trip and lived in Salisbury for a few months and then emigrated to South Africa. I was devastated at losing contact with my children, something I had never anticipated when agreeing to the divorce. However, that marriage was not destined to last. Val returned to Salisbury, or was it Harare by then? What joy in being able to be with my children once more. This joy was short-lived as Val married once again, this time to Robert, the architect who had designed the amazing extensions to our house in Chisipite. Once again Val took the children off to South Africa. I did get to see the youngest from time to time when Val sent him to me during school holidays. The older two were now teenagers and were not inclined to come back to Rhodesia.

Due to stringent exchange control in the country I was not permitted to remit more than a pittance of maintenance for the children to Val in South Africa. I think this fact, more than anything else, resulted in the bitter resentment that Val maintains towards me.

After Val, I dated several women, none of them seriously. Not as far as I was concerned at any rate. There was a certain Ricky who I met through a friend of my mother. (Mother intervening again.) Ricky obviously took our dating far more seriously than I. Once I became aware of this, I promptly stopped taking her out. I only saw her one more time some while later. I had recently remarried and took my new wife to a chic night spot where I bumped into Ricky. I introduced my wife to her which I instantly regretted. Ricky let fly with the most abusive language imaginable calling me all the evil names under the sun and advising my wife to have nothing to do with me.

Alison

I had been serving on our daughter's school PTA (Parent Teachers Association) when I first met Alison. We were both on a team running Tombola for school funds. A few months after Val and I split up we started seeing each other. I discovered how fantastic sex can be when shared with someone you love. There was a major problem. Alison was married and had five children, ages ranging from five to fourteen. I shall not try to play down my role in the breakup of Alison's marriage and I carry the burden of guilt to this day. So much so that I vowed to myself never to come between a married couple again. I mention this because after my marriage to Alison was over, I fell seriously in love again. Ann, also married, was my soulmate from the moment I met her. She qualified as my perfect partner in every way. I was happiest just spending time with her. We played in the same squash team. Even when she was all hot and sweaty, I still thought she was the greatest. Just walking along a beach holding hands filled me with unbelievable happiness and contentment. Perhaps in some ways I still have feelings for her. I certainly still think of her with much fondness. I can say that when the opportunity arose I stuck to my guns and told Ann of my vow. She may have respected me for it; I hope so.

Getting back to Ally, as she was generally known. Ally got a divorce from her husband. He was devastated.

After a respectable period of months had elapsed, Ally said it was time for us to get married. I must confess to having many reservations, mostly regarding her children, as well as the continuous feelings of guilt. And, so it proved. When we got married, I took up residence in her house; another a mistake.

We went on holiday to the Eastern Cape, a belated honeymoon. As we were now a family of seven, I purchased a second-hand VW Kombi. On the way to the coast, just outside Johannesburg on a Sunday and in the remotest place possible, the Kombi broke down. After battling to resolve the problem for over an hour, I decided that I would have to walk ahead to try to find some help. Not one car had passed either way during all that time. After a walk of about two miles I came to a small roadside B&B and asked for assistance to contact a garage or something. I was informed that as it was Sunday, I had no chance. They would be happy to house my family till the next day.

On my way returning to the Kombi to gather everyone for the walk back to the B&B, I came across an African walking in the same direction. He asked me what I was doing in the middle of nowhere and when I related my plight he said he would have a look as he had a little mechanical knowledge. He was better than his word. Within fifteen minutes he had the engine running. (An electrical fault only accessible from under the vehicle.) We were all ecstatic. After giving him a generous tip we set off once more. The engine was not however going to co-operate and started giving trouble again. I had witnessed what my mechanical friend had done to the engine and carried out running repairs which helped for some miles. Every time the engine stopped I became more and more frustrated. The youngest of Ally's boys, Desmond, found it all very entertaining and in his childish way started poking fun at me. This did not help my mood and I told him to stop. Of course, he didn't.

I am ashamed to say I turned around in the car and slapped him across the face. That moment started the end for me.

We eventually arrived at our holiday destination. Hardly a word had been exchanged since that awful moment. The children had by then agreed between themselves not to have anything to do with me. I can't blame them. Poor Ally. She was really caught in the middle. I doubt she realised what was going to happen as neither did I. Over the next few years the children stuck to their guns and virtually froze me out of their lives. We did not even have a polite repartee. The strain on me made me withdraw not only from them but also from Ally, who, bless her, did her utmost to hold the ship together. She was a loving wife as well as a wonderful mother to her children.

I found the next few months were extremely difficult. I made an excuse and informed Ally that my mother was not well. I left for Greece as soon as I could get on a flight. Ally was obviously hurt and, on my return, I duly received the frosty reception which I expected and deserved. I did not let on that while I was in Greece, I met up with Jean, a friend from Zimbabwe. Need I say more?

Ally's children were untidy; I mean, unbelievably untidy; usually leaving clothing and money (pocket money I had given them) on the floor. They never made their beds nor cleared their bedrooms of food plates. (This was no doubt to escape contact with me.) I found myself doing weird things such as picking up the money and putting it back in my pocket. I started avoiding any contact with them, even to the stage of ducking out of sight when I heard one of them approaching. That is really weird! Ally did her best by me and her children but even she felt the strain. The end came whilst on a fishing trip on Kariba dam.

One of my clients had a commercial fishing business and invited Ally and I to spend a weekend with them. Desmond tagged along. The three of us were in one boat, our host and his wife in another. I was disappointed that Desmond had decided to come along for the trip; this at a time I needed to spend with my wife trying to fathom a way through the woods. The two boats were in close proximity. As luck would have it, Ally and Desmond got bored and started splashing the water and banging on the bottom of the boat, much to everyone else's annoyance. I decide it best to depart and reeled in my line. Ally asked if I had had enough.

I could not help myself. "Yes! I have had enough. I have had more than enough," I blurted out.

It was now my turn to seek advice from a psychiatrist. He informed me I was suffering from acute environmental depression. There was only one possible remedy. That was for me 'to get out'. The moment he said it I felt a huge weight lift from my shoulders.

And thus, ended my second marriage of four mostly unhappy years. I kept in touch with Ally though the damage was irreparable. It is a pity that a relationship which started out so full of promise should end in a manner which left us both feeling we had failed. After I had moved out, she did her best to bring the family together again. At one point, I actually relented and returned to her house. It took a full five minutes in the company of her children for me to realise things would never change. I was making a huge mistake; I kissed her on the cheek and walked away. Poor Ally. Poor me. We never stood a chance!

Once again, I was welcomed as a lodger by Joy Yeatman. She never once intervened in my affairs or tried to give me advice. She accepted me as I was for which I will always be grateful.

After I married Brenda and our two babes were at a walking stage, I took them to see Joy. We visited her quite regularly. When she died some years later, I was surprised at the emotion her loss left me with; a true friend.

Brenda

I met Brenda when I joined the Palmer group way back in 1973. She was manager of one of Palmer's car hire companies. At the time, I regarded her as an attractive, fun loving and competent person and as the business she managed was one of the few making money, she was kept on until I found a buyer for the business some months later. She was not married and lived with a partner, James. They were both avid horse racing fans. Val and I enjoyed a social life with them for a while, playing cards and going out to restaurants. I am not sure when or why we went our separate ways.

I met up with Brenda some years later. I had joined Round Table and she was then living with another man in the same club. Round Table membership ceases at the age of 40; i.e. in my case in 1977. I lost touch with her once again.

It was no surprise to me when I bumped into Brenda at the race course in 1985. Joy, my landlady, was a regular visitor to the track and frequently invited me to accompany her. I had lost my interest in betting on horse racing years earlier. The reason for this will be related later.

We dated for a short while during which I guess I became besotted with her. This adoration rather put her off me and I eventually took the hint. All my friends kept setting me up with dates. I was playing a lot of squash at the time and met Sue on the squash court. We started going out regularly and enjoyed similar interests. Sue was another who spent time at the horse races. I was once again lodging at Joy Yeatman's house, so became a regular visitor to the race course. Yet once again, I met Brenda at the course and was surprised to discover my feelings for Brenda were still very much alive. By now Sue and I had become quite close, a fact that did not escape Brenda. I found myself being pursued by two lovely persons, perhaps for the first time in my life, and was quite unsure of myself. I was uncomfortable with being emotionally involved with both girls as I am not a 'gigolo' by nature. Things came to a head when Brenda suggested that we should try to make a go of it. My relationship with Sue was one of comfortable togetherness, but no long-term plans had been discussed. My telling Sue I was breaking off our relationship was perhaps the most uncomfortable decision I have ever made. It devastated her as it did me. We hugged and cried together as if the world was at an end; for us; it had. Very hard on us both, but I walked away.

I did not move in with Brenda. We grew to know and respect each other's space. She lived in her house and I had added living accommodation to a house which also housed my offices. Brenda was learning to play the piano, something I too wished to do. She told me that the best thing would be for me to buy a piano. I did. I now had to add yet another small room onto the house for the piano.

For a whole year, I went weekly for piano lessons. At that time my work load had increased significantly and I was having problems finding sufficient time to practice. When I arrived for a lesson which proved to be the last, I was as tense as a violin string, had a severe headache and the shirt I had on was bathed in perspiration. I decide enough was enough and called an end to my piano lessons. Nevertheless; I could now read music and could play popular tunes, though, not particularly well. Today, nothing has changed. I try to find time to play and always enjoy the time I spend at that very same piano. All thanks to Brenda.

We dated exclusively, went on lots of holidays and made

love. And, in due course, you guessed it, she fell pregnant.

In December 1986 my eldest son, Gray, married Anita in Johannesburg. I am a very private person and had not mentioned being in a relationship with Brenda to anyone. The looks I got when I pitched up at the wedding with a very pregnant girlfriend, I leave to your imagination. In passing, I mention that Val was obviously at the wedding and had known Brenda many years back. She was speechless.

Our son, Simon, was born on the 4th March 1987. Many years later, I discovered that his great, great grandfather, James Beazley mentioned at the start of my family history, was also born on this day. I know there are only 365 days in a year, so the odds are not that overwhelming, but I am amazed how so many 'same days' have significance in my life.

I married Brenda on 22nd of March 1985 in the garden of her lovely house. I had moved in on a permanent basis a few days earlier. Not only did we get married that day; it was also Brenda's birthday and Simon was christened as well. Lots and lots of friends, lots of laughs and lots of champagne. After all we were celebrating three memorable occasions. I commenced my speech to my new wife and our friends with the opening words; "Accustomed as I am becoming…"

It was one of the very best days of my life.

I have failed to mention that once again I was sporting a black eye. This, on my wedding day! A shareholder in a public company for which we acted as secretaries had pledged his holding to a bank on a loan. The bank duly called up the loan and the shares were transferred to the bank. Due to bad timing we were in the process of sending dividend cheques to registered shareholders; in this case, the individual. He banked his cheque but not before we noticed our mistake and put a stop on the cheque. I, as the owner of my trust company, was confronted by a very angry man. He was not interested in my explanation and landed a blow on my eye as I sat at my desk. When I stood up to fight back he realised that I was much bigger than him and withdrew a nasty looking knife from his jacket. I shouted out to my secretary in the adjoining room that he had a knife and to call the police. He ran out the office but returned within a minute to continue arguing but there was no sign of the knife. The police arrived within minutes, heard my story, and did a body search on the man for the knife. Needless to say, they did not find one. I was too shocked to think clearly. He must have disposed of the knife when he ran out of the office, something I thought about later.

He was taken away by the police and jailed for attacking me. A day or so later a senior police officer called on me and requested that I drop the charge as the man was a high ranking political figure in Mugabe's henchmen. I had little choice as I regularly undertook investigations into corruption for the government. I agreed with the proviso that this man would never again bother me, my family and my staff. I will mention in passing that this same man was arrested a few months later, on a murder charge. With hindsight, it could have been so much worse.

Life with Brenda was exceptionally good. We made an early trip to England to visit Brenda's family, who had been unable to travel to Zimbabwe for the wedding. During that holiday, we took her parents for a week's break to Newquay. This was my first experience of the English seaside and turned out much better than I had expected. I love swimming in the sea and found the temperature of the water warm enough to spend some time in it. What did catch me by complete surprise was the speed and strength of the tides. We had sat Brenda's parents in deck chairs at the top end of the beach and then walked some way down to the water. We took Simon with us, still a babe in arms. When I noticed the tide had turned, we headed back to the old folks. Brenda's dad was classified as a blind man and her mother was a simple and trusting soul.

Imagine my shock when we finally got back to them. They were still seated in their deck chairs with the swirling sea now almost to their knees. They had not budged!

There was one other 'spooky event' I recall from that holiday. I had been exploring the rocks while the tide was out and came upon a travel bag placed, or should I say, hidden between the rocks. I could not see anyone nearby and proceeded to look in the bag. It contained two wrapped presents and a rather tattered diary. The diary stated it belonged to Margaret *****. The last words in the diary were 'Sorry'. It was only then I spotted a rather sharp knife under the presents. I took the bag back up the beach to a group of elderly ladies chatting on the grass and enquired whether any of them was Margaret *****. One of the women said Margaret had been there earlier and offered to return the bag to her. It is only recently that I have tried to make sense of what it was all about. Perhaps, ignorance is bliss.

We had a second child two years later and I like to believe we were both happy. I certainly was. We had a grand extension built onto the house as well as an all-weather tennis court. We played bridge together, which was a first for me as Val wouldn't and Ally couldn't. We had a very nice circle of friends and many weekends were spent holding tennis combined with bridge parties. The children and their friends were well cared for. We had a large garden with a swimming pool. And, of course, we all had lots of domestic help. The boys learnt to swim at an early age (from two years on) as did most youngsters. Simon had a very competitive streak in him and at an early age was swimming for a club and provincially. The other thing Brenda had him doing was BMX cycling. Again, very competitive and lots of trophies. Jason, on the other hand, hated swimming and always complained bitterly that he was cold when he had swimming lessons

Do all good things need to come to an end? It seems so.

In September 1994 Brenda collapsed having experienced an aneurysm. I must commend the medical team in Harare. Their response to my panic call was fast and she was in hospital within an hour. I asked Melody, my sister living in Athens, to come out to help with the boys. Brenda hated the hospital and requested her physician to permit her to go home. Apart from having a problem with her eyes and a slight headache she seemed ok. We were all delighted to have her back with us. A week later she had another aneurysm and died in the early hours of the next morning. Even as I write these words I am experiencing intense grief and my eyes are full of tears. (This is some twenty two years later. It has caught me by complete surprise.)

Simon, now seven, took the loss of his mother particularly badly, Jason, being two years younger, seemed to cope the best of the three of us. But life has to go on. At the time, I was chairman of the boys' school PTA. The support I received from that quarter and indeed so many of our friends was overwhelming. I needed to sort out our day-to-day lives and so engaged the services of a Mrs. Doubtfire, an elderly Irish carer who drove all three of us nuts. We were given a thin slice of toasted cucumber with an anchovy for lunch almost every day. Nothing else. One day, while collecting the boys from nursery school, she drove my motor car into a petrol pump while filling up. My Mercedes was never the same after that.

Shortly before her death Brenda had planned a seaside holiday and we had ordered a new VW Caravelle in which to make the long trip to the coast. It arrived after Brenda had passed away and after the accident to my car at the petrol pump. So, I was now able to offload the damaged Mercedes.

Wendy

The holiday Brenda had planned was to a resort in the Transkei very near to the last holiday I had spent with Val. I hated the thought of driving a new vehicle along that dreadful road. And now that Brenda was gone I decided to cancel the holiday. However, our friends persuaded me to go for the sake of the boys. I relented and shortly before Christmas set off for the coast. As expected the road was in an awful state of disrepair. I was feeling very sorry for myself. I envisaged sitting alone at a table for meals as the boys would have to eat their meals in the children's dining room. And so it proved for a day or two.

Wendy and her daughter Natalie, aged six, had been invited to join some friends on their holiday as another couple, who were due to join them, had backed out. It proved that she too was unattached and in fact we were the only persons at the resort (excluding children),who were single.

My philosophy in life has always been fatalistic. I accept what life throws my way and do my best to get on with it. The timing of the arrival of Wendy in my life could not have been more perfect. Here was a lovely, talented, energetic young lady who, though eighteen years my junior, decided to take us into her life and accept us just the way we were. I am not too sure whether Natalie was that keen on the idea. From my point of view, I could not think of anyone I would rather entrust my children to, particularly after my Mrs. Doubtfire experience. Though she lived in Johannesburg, I did not feel a move to South Africa was too difficult an undertaking even though I knew that South Africa had a very serious security problem.

Wendy and Natalie were invited to come to Harare to inspect our standard of life in case she had been carried away by the moment whilst on holiday. It did not take long for us both to conclude we wanted to be together. It was decided that I would settle the boys with Wendy in Johannesburg and that I would commute between there and Harare thereby continuing my business activities. I flew down to Johannesburg every Thursday afternoon and returned to Harare for work early Monday morning. Wendy set about finding a house that would accommodate us all and enable her to pursue her business interests as a conference organiser. In March, a month in which all three children celebrate their respective birthdays, each one year apart, Wendy advised me she had found an ideal home for us.

I arrived at the airport one Thursday afternoon and was met by Wendy but not in her usual motorcar. She had been hijacked whilst in her car parked right outside the home we were in the process of purchasing. This house had maximum security, including a seven foot high paling fence, topped by electric wiring, concertina gates on all doors, Spanish bars on all windows and panic buttons situated strategically throughout. The only problem was that Wendy was parked outside of the front gate. The four hijackers blocked her escape by parking their getaway vehicle behind Wendy's car. They banged on her side window brandishing guns and knives and told her not to look at them and to get out or they would kill her. And all this for a VW Golf. They also took the jewellery she had with her including an emerald engagement ring I had placed on her finger the previous week.

I can tell you that Wendy's nerves were shattered. We attempted to put things right by getting thoroughly drunk that evening.

We purchased a new car (Honda Ballade) and installed a security system in the vehicle, which entails pressing and flicking several controls on the dashboard. If the sequence was not strictly adhered to, the car could not be driven. As I was in Johannesburg on Fridays, it was my duty to get the children to school. On one occasion, I experienced some difficulty but did manage finally to start the car. After driving a mile from home the engine stopped, the headlights started flashing and the horn set off a series of continuous loud blasts. This served to notify the nearby house dwellers that a car in the near vicinity was being stolen. Armed response teams arrived in minutes and it took some time for me to convince them that I had not stolen my own car. They escorted me back to our house and only when I produced the plug to disarm the immobilizer did they accept my explanation.

I managed to disconnect the horn but could not stop the headlights flashing. That afternoon I collected the children from school and was driving home when a big black four-by-four forced me off the road. I thought I was being hijacked. It was only when I heard the driver of the other car calling the police for assistance as he had intercepted a hijacker that I saw the funny side and started laughing uncontrollably. Once again, I had to explain why I was driving a car with flashing lights.

On the 9th April 1995, we tied the knot. We had a civil wedding in the morning and Wendy organised a reception for our families and friends at a garden nursery in the evening. Apart from the rain that poured down on us as we arrived at the reception, the evening was quite splendid. Several of my friends from Zimbabwe made the trip as had my, now aging, mother. Wendy believes she has Scottish blood in her and even organised a piper to escort us into the venue. Natalie was in tears, but not of joy. She had stepped into a deep puddle and her ballet pumps she wore for the occasion were soaked.

From 1995 to the middle of 1997 we grew together as a family. We managed to fit in plenty of holidays, sometimes to the seaside, others to game reserves. All our trips were wonderful fun and though there are numerous stories of our time in South Africa, there is one that I think you will find amusing.

Wendy ran her business from our home. She was a conference organiser and took us all on an inspection trip for a conference she was in the process of organising.

The trip was out to sea and back on a luxury liner over three days. I have always been a terrible sailor, even getting seasick rowing on a dam. I took my pills and was fine. Wendy claimed never to get seasick. Ha. Ha. On the first night out, she had to lie prone on her bed in our cabin. But she is a very determined young lady and the following morning she set about doing her inspection. I and the boys dressed in our evening best, believing it was Captain's night. Of course, we got that wrong. We were the only ones smartly dressed that night; all the other diners wore casuals.

Our first overseas trip was to England, where we stayed at my sister's apartment in Pont Street, London. The children were now aged six, seven and eight. While Wendy went to explore the shops I decided to take the children to the nearby museum on a cultural trip. Wendy had bought the children Kipling backpacks and we set off on our own exploration. After a couple of hours, we took a tea break. I then noticed Jason no longer had his backpack. A quick lecture from me and then we backtracked trying to locate the pack. After another hour of frustration, it suddenly dawned on me that Jason had never had his Kipling pack with him. We were now exhausted and decided to call it a day. Outside, it had started raining. I hailed a taxi and instructed our driver to set off for 52 Pont Street.

In the apartment, sure enough there we found Jason's backpack. It was then that Simon informed me that he no longer had his, having left it in the taxi. I was beside myself with annoyance and proceeded to deliver another lecture on the importance of being responsible for one's possessions. Wendy chose that moment to return from her shopping trip. I shall not repeat her language when she was told the news. It ended with instructions to Simon and me to go outside and check whether the pack may have fallen out of the taxi and on to the pavement. The two of us rushed to escape the verbal onslaught. Down the stairs we went, striding towards the front door. And then I could hardly believe my eyes. In a cage which was designed to collect mail for all the tenants, was Simon's backpack! The taxi driver must have found it in his cab, and delivered it back to the address where he had dropped us. Unbelievable! My faith in the human race had never been higher and my opinion of all London taxi drivers will be held in the highest regard for the remaining years of my life.

Regrettably, I do not have the same regard for our police. We moved to live in England in 2000. One morning some years later, before 7.00a.m. I awoke to a loud thumping on our front door. Bearing in mind we had a perfectly working electric bell on the door, the thumping seemed quite unnecessary. I staggered downstairs, barely awake, in my pyjamas and opened the door where I was confronted by two very well built, uniformed young policemen. In an extremely aggressive manner they demanded to know if I was Jason Beazley. I informed them that I was not and Jason was my youngest son who at that moment was at university in Portsmouth. They virtually pushed their way into my house and demanded to conduct a search of the property. I requested sight of a warrant upon which they became even more aggressive. I asked them to explain what business they had with Jason and was rudely informed that it was none of my business. I advised them that as Jason was still under the age of 18, as his parent I was entitled to know. (I confess not being too sure of my rights but felt it necessary to show some resistance.)

I was told that they could obtain a warrant and while the one officer set about getting this the other would remain on my premises to ensure Jason, or anyone else, did not leave the property. I waived the need to obtain a warrant as it seemed a waste of time to delay the matter further. The policemen then rushed around the house both up and down stairs, opening cupboards, looking under beds and even conducted their search to the garden. Once they were satisfied that Jason was not on the property they departed. I advised them I would be reporting the matter but they could not have cared less.

I did report the incident to my Member of Parliament and full marks to him, he took the matter up with the Police

Commissioner. After an investigation and some months, I received a letter of apology from the police. Sometime later I found out that all they wanted was to question Jason as he had been a witness to a verbal 'racial exchange'. I will never understand the heavy-handed manner of those policemen. It has left me with a lasting impression of 'police brutality'. Such a pity and so short-sighted to besmirch the reputation of our hard-working force. Even in trouble torn Zimbabwe, police officers behave in a more civilized manner. Having seen several scenes of police behaviour on the television over the years, I suppose the incident could have got worse.

I fear I have again digressed; so back to experiences with Wendy.

A friend of mine from Zimbabwe owned a holiday home at a seaside resort in the Eastern Cape called Kenton. The five of us, together with Wendy's sister, her husband and two children and Granny (Wendy and Jeannie's mother) enjoyed a very nice beach holiday there. The bathing was very safe for the children and Kenton is located near other resorts which we visited. Kenton is bounded to the east by quite a wide river. A group of university students had organised a camp in the bush up the river which was reported to serve amazing meals. The food on offer was BBQ style or Braai as it is known in South Africa. One student, who we named Captain Ron, had a large pontoon on which he transported visitors to the campsite. Later when everyone had dined and wined, he would return the visitors back to the landing at Kenton.

As I recall the food was indeed outstanding. It included fish, game and a variety of meats. The salads were delicious. When our five youngsters grew weary around 10 p.m., we requested Captain Ron to take us back. It was a very dark night and the tide had turned so the river was now actively flowing into the sea. I would hazard a guess that we were, in all probability, experiencing a spring tide. As we neared the Kenton landing,

Captain Ron grabbed a thin rope, jumped onto the landing and endeavoured to pull the pontoon next to the landing so that we could alight.

We all heard the rope snap. Captain Ron emitted a loud "Oh Shit" as he watched his beloved pontoon with the ten of us being swept out to sea! Possibly never to be seen again!

George, Jean's husband, grabbed the engine's control lever and thrust it into reverse while I pulled at the rudder in an attempt to steer the pontoon back to the landing. Needless to say we failed. But we were successful enough to beach the pontoon on some nearby rocks badly scraping the bottom of the pontoon in the process. The pontoon was now lying at a sixty degree angle with the lower part sitting in rapid flowing seawater. Somehow we managed to get everyone safely off. My last recollection of the night was hearing Captain Ron muttering to himself on the loss of his pontoon. I sometimes wonder if he ever considers how the episode might have ended.

As the months rolled over it became clear to us that South Africa was not the ideal place in which to raise our children. We considered Australia but in the end were persuaded by my sister to have a look at Cyprus. Before we left South Africa, we all made one last trip to Zimbabwe. We visited the usual holiday resorts and game parks. We also visited a gold mine which happened to belong to a John Cinamon. This same man featured in my very first insolvency case way back in 1975. He also turned out to be a relative of Wendy's, being a cousin of her mother. This really is a small world. Some months later, he became a victim of the government's economic empowerment for the indigenous population. John was forced off his gold mine and had to flee the country. He and his wife came to England where Wendy once again met up with them in Skegness.

I mentioned earlier that Wendy operated in business as an event organiser. During our years together she has organised and planned two major events. The first was in respect of my

70th birthday. She located a large farm house in the Tewksbury area. Here most of my family from near and far met up for a week of country living. The centre of activities revolved around the kitchen. This was a large room with a very long dining table able to seat us all. Wendy organised teams of two to take daily turns in planning and preparing the meals. The same applied to the daily entertainment program.

Tewksbury experienced the worst flooding in its recent history that year. Our activities were therefore mostly confined to the farm house. At the end of the week I was aware of a certain good feeling of comradeship in the family, which left us all with that warm glow of time, well spent together. I cannot recall even one heated exchange between any of us.

The second event was in respect of Wendy's 60th. She hired a castle in Scotland for the week. Once again the family assembled along with some close friends. Craigrownie Castle boasts several magnificent lounges, a dining room with a long oak table and hand carved oak chairs, and eleven stately bedrooms. The castle was lavishly furnished and decorated. Wendy and I slept in a huge four-poster bed with a surprisingly comfortable mattress.

Once again the weather was unkind but it mattered not. Wendy organised our entertainment on a splendid scale. The night before her birthday was devoted to a murder mystery. She rewrote the script and had acquired props to dress each person for their respective part in the play. I could not get over how fantastically everyone contributed to the fun; even the most reserved came to the fore. The only 'disappointment' to the evening was my being the murderer; something I did not expect as I faithfully read my lines.

Kitchen duties were once again shared though this time with some assistance from 'Rose' (Waitrose.) The birthday party was a Scottish affair. We all wore something with a tartan theme. We even took to the floor with some Scottish dancing. Wendy's boss sponsored a piper and when the haggis came in to the party, her boss, in full dress for the occasion, proceeded to 'slaughter' it with his dirk and much gusto.

We even had time to do some sightseeing later in the week. A visit to a whiskey distillery has introduced me to the pleasure of having a sip accompanied by a nibble of fudge.

Some five years ago, Wendy bought a flower shop in the village of Redbourn. The plan would be that once the business generated enough income, Wendy would resign from her 8.30 to 5.30 job and devote her full time to the shop. The shop never grew to the size she had hoped for. She is still involved but has brought in a partner with the intention of selling off her remaining interest once her landlord's lease had run its full course.

My involvement in the venture was confined to flower delivery services and keeping the books. I cannot overstate how much pleasure I got from delivering the arrangements. One delivery service, in particular, brought me tons of enjoyment. Dan was making approaches to a very attractive school teacher named Charlotte. My first delivery made 24 days before Christmas was to deliver a solitary red rose without any note to Charlotte at the school where she taught. This was a considerable distance from Redbourn but hey, Dan was paying! The next day I delivered a single white rose, still no note, and deliveries alternated between red and white day by day. When the school term ended for the Christmas break I had to deliver the daily rose to Charlotte's residence, which happened to be a few hundred yards from our home.

Charlotte had a wicked sense of humour and our daily contact became quite special. She began with "Romeo, Romeo, wherefore art thou?" The next day I sang, "Only a rose, I bring you." Charlotte vowed to go into competition with our flower shop as she was accumulating 'lots of roses'. Each day there was some form of banter; great fun. Finally, on Christmas Eve I delivered 24 red and white roses. This time, a note accompanied the flowers. It simply asked Charlotte to marry him, Dan.

They were married a year later; we provided the flowers.

As time went on, I made many friends. I delivered flowers year after year to the same people. Birthdays, anniversaries, Mothers' Day, Christmas time and my favourite; Valentine's Day. I must mention one regular recipient; Sylvia. What a lovely, friendly and warm person. My delivery duties have now ended; I shall miss her.

6

Cyprus (1997-2000)

In September 1996, we holidayed in Greece and on returning to South Africa made our decision to leave the country. Our first thoughts were toward Australia. On hearing this news, my sister pleaded with us to have a look at Cyprus. Wendy met Melody in Paphos in October and at the end of two weeks informed me that we were now the owners of a plot of land situated in the Tala district. Not only that, she had engaged the services of a developer and the two had designed our home. I first saw the house under construction in Easter 1997 and was thrilled with our 180 degree view of the sunset. The plot was on the side of a mountain with an unrestricted view of the sea; absolutely stunning.

And so it came about. In August 1997 we arrived in Paphos in the early hours of the morning. Our house was all but ready for our arrival. The developer, Costas Gavrilides, let us have use of an apartment in Paphos he had recently constructed, for the few days needed before we could take occupation.

And so to sleep.

I was the first to arise around nine that morning having got to sleep at 3.00 a.m. Wendy got up shortly after. There was certainly a buzz of excitement and anticipation in the air. Wendy went to check on the children and found Simon still fast asleep in one bedroom. The next bedroom though, was empty. No sign of Natalie or Jason. She asked me whether I had seen them and of course I had not. I did a quick scout outside to no avail.

I have mentioned earlier that Wendy's nerves were shattered after her hijacking. Panic set in right away. Here we were in a strange town and land and there was no sign of our two youngest. We phoned Costas who appeared within a short space of time. He and I drove around Paphos looking for two children. Talk about a needle in a haystack! Needless to say, we returned to the apartment empty-handed. Wendy had stayed behind just in case the children found their way back.

Around mid-morning Costas received a call on his mobile and was informed that two small children were at the caller's house. The little girl kept repeating the name of Gavrilides. What a clever girl! Natalie had somehow remembered hearing us speak of Costas by his surname and the name had stuck. I am sure she could not have heard it more than five or six times. The youngsters had woken early and gone exploring. The streets of Paphos are not set out in rectangles but twist and turn. When they could not find their way back to the apartment, they had ambled along the streets until they found a living body who could fathom their plight. Just another little adventure.

We moved into our new home a few days later. I must confess that during those early days I felt I had arrived in Heaven. Everything was great. Swimming in the sea was wonderful. The food was wonderful (apart from coriander which I cannot stand). Cyprus is highly anglicised. Most of the Cypriots have more than a smattering of English; certainly more than our Greek. Before leaving South Africa, we went for weekly Greek lessons. Accordingly, Wendy addressed a supermarket attendant in her very best Greek only to be told "Please speak to me in English, Madam."

Driving is on the left and generally the people are friendly and helpful. Or so I thought in the beginning. Regrettably my opinion changed over the months as I woke up to the fact that they were there to take foreigners to the cleaners. My eyes were in fact opened within a few days of our arrival. I purchased a TV system from a recommended dealer, only to find it beamed out a signal from a middle-east station. The result was that the children watching programs before bedtime had a wonderful view of belly dancers and sights considerably more for adult viewing.

When I complained bitterly to the dealer he refused to budge on any exchange of programming box until I accused him of taking gross advantage of me. This resulted in a prompt about turn and we were given a box tuned into a local station. Why not in the first place?

It was only a short while later that I woke up to the fact that foreigners were fair game by the majority of the locals whom I generally classified as having a village mentality.

I was still working in Zimbabwe and commuted on a three week at a time basis; i.e. three weeks in Paphos and three weeks in Harare. On my first trip back to Paphos, I fulfilled one of the items on my bucket list. I bought a 22 foot long boat which I named Scorpios. I was allocated a mooring site in a small harbour and secured Scorpios with a large slab of concrete which I made with my very own hands. Not bad for an office type. On my next return to Paphos, I went to my mooring site only to find my boat was not there and a local fisherman had secured his boat onto my concrete slab. I located my boat drifting in the next bay, completely unsecured. Fortunately, the Cypriot summers produce few storms and there was no damage. I returned my boat to my mooring.

I regret to say that I experienced the same treatment every time until I eventually decide to pull my boat from the water and park her at home. This meant launching Scorpios whenever I used the boat. Nevertheless, we had many great times in the boat and were able to entertain numerous friends who came to see us.

I am a keen fisherman but never caught one fish during our three years in Cyprus. I confess to finding out that my duties of ensuring everyone on board was safe at all times quite stressful and my enjoyment waned somewhat. Shortly before leaving the island I found a buyer for Scorpios. There is a time worn saying that the two best days of your life are, firstly, when you buy your boat and secondly when you sell it.

Harare and Cyprus are on the same line of longitude so there is no time change involved; I used to leave Harare about seven o'clock in the evening and arrive in Cyprus at Larnica airport around two o'clock the next morning. A highlight of my life has been looking out on the right side of the aircraft window and gazing in absolute awe at the wonderful beauty of the Nile River. It is illuminated by lights all along its banks for hundreds of miles. Absolutely spectacular!

In 1998 my second son Nick got married in Johannesburg and my sister and I travelled to South Africa to attend the wedding. We arrived at the church on time along with many other guests. There we sat. And sat. And sat. No sign of the bride. Gray, my eldest son, was due to bring the bride to the church. That morning he had taken delivery of a spanking new BMW. When it came to leave for the church he could not start the engine. Being a Saturday afternoon he was unable to locate the car dealer. It was only an hour later he made contact and was informed how to release the immobilizer. Did I mention we waited and waited?

After the ceremony, we assembled at the reception venue and duly waited for the entrance of the bride and groom. And we waited. And we waited. And we waited. Finally, after almost an hour the couple entered the hall. Nick wore an evening suit, while Leanne wore a stunning full length wedding dress. I was placed next to one of the bridesmaids and asked her "Why the delay?" She informed me that the lower half of the wedding dress was supported by a cage-like structure. Before entering the hall, Leanne wished to use the loo. However, she was not able to remove her undies as the cage prevented her from doing so. The bridesmaid then performed the task by climbing under the cage. After Leanne had done what she had to do, the bridesmaid had to, once again, replace the undies. To add to the time delay I was informed that the bridesmaid's hair had become entangled in the cage. The rest of the night went off without any more problems. The happy couple and their attendants performed an extremely good dance routine for our entertainment.

One Friday, I arrived at Harare's airport only to be informed that Mugabe had grabbed the plane and that I would be flying to London that night. Arrangements were being made for me to get from London to Cyprus. No problem? There was a problem.

Zimbabwe's beef is second to none. Each time I travelled to Cyprus I would stuff my suitcase with frozen fillets. Normally, when I arrived at our house in Paphos some ten hours later, these fillets were still frozen.

On arrival in London early on Saturday morning, I found the same Zimbabwe plane I had arrived on would carry me to Frankfurt. Sure enough I arrived at Frankfurt at midday. End of the line. The next plane to Cyprus departed 24 hours later (on Sunday). As I had no need for toiletries, clean clothes or money, I always travelled light i.e. one large suitcase in the hold of the plane. As we were only in transit in Germany we were not permitted to collect our luggage. I was not a happy bunny. I could not even buy a Coca Cola at the hotel we were placed at for the night. Also, never ever drink Frankfurt's tap water!

Next morning, off to the airport. There were 34 passengers in transit. We were informed that the plane going to Cyprus only had seats for 15 persons. As my surname starts with 'B', I was one of the lucky ones. I arrived at Larnica airport in Cyprus shortly before dark. Guess what. No suitcase. On Monday night shortly before 11p.m. I received a call advising me that my suitcase had been found and would be delivered shortly. I was panicking and imagined that there would be blood pouring out of the suitcase and I would be suspected of having it contain a body. The suitcase was delivered at 2.30 a.m. some 84 hours after I had filled it with frozen meat in Harare. Yes, there was a fair amount of blood which had fortunately been absorbed by items of clothing. And yes, my case reeked of kippers which I had also placed in the case. I was surprised, however, to find the fillets still cool and perfectly fine to consume.

There were several other unfavourable incidents which soured my feelings for the island. On one occasion a friend was coming to dine with us. To get to the village of Tala one has to drive up a long hilly road. Our friend was proceeding slowly up this hill when suddenly a young Russian girl jumped into the path of our friend's car. She was not injured but cried out in Russian, in apparent agony. It was clearly a staged accident and this was confirmed by some witnesses. The police were called and took statements after which our friend was permitted to go in the belief that she had no case to answer. Two weeks later she was charged with negligent driving and causing bodily harm to the Russian. She only averted a jail sentence by paying a hefty fine for damages. I wonder how much of the fine the police retained and how much went to the young lady.

I, too, was involved with the police. We had obtained a permit for a very pleasant, hard working Philippine girl to work for us. Leonila proved to be a real gem. She was great with the children, worked endless hours in the house and garden, cleaned the car, washed the dogs. I could go on extolling her virtues but I am sure you get the picture. One day, I took Leonila to clean a friend's villa. I was on the beach when I received a call from the police telling me that they had our maid in custody. To cut to the chase, she was being charged with working illegally. I took full responsibility advising them that I had instructed her to do the cleaning. I produced the work permit but the police maintained that the permit only related to cleaning our house and not to other places. This was not specified on the permit but there was no budging the police. I expect they were looking to me to produce a wad of money. Leonila was released on bail, the next day. Why they had to detain her overnight is a mystery.

A few days later I received papers with charges against Leonila and myself. Apparently I, too, had broken the law; twice. Once for making Leonila work in a place other than our house and secondly, by driving her to our friend's villa I was deemed to be working, which was illegal as I did not have a permit to work in Cyprus. It was clear that we both were in trouble. It was also clear that Leonila was facing a prison sentence. I did the only thing possible. I sent her back to the Philippines. In due course, I appeared in court and was fined £500 on the two counts. My lawyer was quite useless and would not put up any defence on my behalf.

This same lawyer had processed all the documents for the purchase of our plot in Tala. When we came to sell our property on leaving Cyprus it transpired that we had no title to the land. And even later after we had sold up, the purchaser of our house retained funds until the land title had been cleared. I was now living in England and had little success in contacting our lawyer who was always unavailable. I had no choice but to travel back to the island. When I confronted the lawyer he virtually told me to go home as he had decided I was no longer his client. He would do nothing further to clear up his mess. It took another year and another lawyer to complete the transfer.

Wendy also had a fair share of problems. Our children attended an international school. She and another mother promoted drama, music and other non-academic activities. The headmistress of the school took exception to their involving themselves in her domain. All rather difficult.

The school did not cater for sixth form education. We

made the decision to move to England to ensure the children had the opportunity of attending university. Harpenden in Hertfordshire had three high schools with excellent reputations. This crystalized our thoughts and the move was made. Not all smooth sailing as all three children were allocated to different schools. I had no choice but to appeal to the authorities to place the children together. I overheard the interview of the appellant before me which ended in a shouting match and no satisfactory conclusion. I was concerned that I, too, would not have a satisfactory outcome. The appeal board could not have been more understanding once I related the loss of the boys' mother and Wendy's hijacking. All three were granted a place in the same school.

Cyprus was not all bad. We made some good friends and regularly see a few of these. We have been back to the island since it joined the EU. This has led to a sharp increase in inflation. We found prices had rocketed and were extremely relieved to have moved to England when we did.

7

Children

I cannot stress how much all my children mean to me. It is therefore fitting that I devote some words to them.

My eldest, Gray, suffered for that very reason; he was the firstborn and experienced all the difficulties attributed to that roll. The most lasting memory I have of Gray as a child was his determination to please his parents in everything he did. I recall playing football with him in our garden. The ball sat up inviting me to kick, which I did with force. Gray was in goal and the ball struck him full on in the face. He did his utmost not to cry. My brave little soldier; I felt so much love for him in that moment. On another occasion at school sports, Val and I entered a parents' egg and spoon race. We did not win; Gray was distraught and berated the two of us for not trying harder. I do not know where such will to succeed came from; certainly, not from me.

Over the years, it became apparent that he would be our 'difficult' child; the rebel. I grew to accept him as he was. Academically, he was not the top student but his artistic talents were superb. I wonder whether the art teacher, a pretty young thing, had something to do with his excellence. Rumour has it that they were an 'item' in his final school year. On another occasion, when he was fifteen, a very angry father swept into my office demanding I find his daughter. She had not been home for three days and was shacked up with Gray somewhere in Salisbury. It took me most of the day to track them down.

Many years later once he was living on his own, I agreed to spend a weekend with him in his apartment in Johannesburg. (I was still living in Zimbabwe.) The weekend passed without any major upset apart from my having to sleep on the carpet in his sitting room. The carpet stank of cat's pee!

Gray had recently broken up with his girlfriend. On my last night, he went to see her with a promise that he would return in plenty of time to get me to the city airport terminal the next morning. Lying on that smelly carpet, I just knew he was going to let me down. And so it transpired. I had a large suitcase full of luxury items unavailable in Rhodesia. At 5.00a.m. I decided I would have to lug this heavy case through the streets for two miles to the terminal. I was not a happy bunny. Fortunately, an early riser driving past saw me struggling along the pavement and gave me a lift. I got to the terminal just as the bus was about to depart for the airport. I would never have made it on my own.

That night, back safely in my home, Gray phoned with profuse apologies. I was surprised that I had no feelings of annoyance or resentment. I had anticipated he would not pitch and I accepted it just like that. No damage to our relationship.

Gray has done really well for himself. He and his wife own and run a fantastic boutique hotel in Johannesburg. They produced two granddaughters for me, also involved in running 'The Oasis'.

My daughter, Penny, turned out to be the intelligent one; always had her head screwed on correctly. Even in matters of the heart she was always sensible. She had this boyfriend who I found 'unsuitable', mainly because I regarded his intellectual level being far below Penny's. (I sound like my mother!) The relationship seemed to be progressing until one day, her boyfriend told her he was getting married the following month to someone else. Naturally, Penny was very upset. I was relieved.

It was only a couple of months later that this fellow, now married, came calling on Penny saying he had made a terrible mistake. My sensible daughter sent him packing. Just as well, as this chap got involved with an African business man, who landed them both in jail. Penny moved to Toronto, Canada shortly after. I have been for a visit; found Toronto a highly organised city. While I was there, we went to Algonquin where a chipmunk ran up my jeans and into my pocket; reminiscent of the African squirrel. I had not expected chipmunks to be so small.

Penny has never married; a shame, as I think she would have been good at raising children. She has had an on/off relationship with someone who seemed to be after her money.

Nick is the quiet one; serious, but not to a fault. He was a good student and has two university degrees. He is now a consultant in air-conditioning, mainly for the mines. He and his wife have one son, my grandson and also live in South Africa. I regret I do not get to see much of any of my three elder children and my three grandchildren.

It is quite the opposite with my two younger boys and my step-daughter. After completing their university degrees, the boys decided there was no place like home. So, until recently we have had three mid-twenty year olds sharing our space and our lives. I must confess to enjoying having had them around. Simon moved out a year ago. Jason moved out six months ago but has recently come back. Natalie has only recently left the nest to move in to her newly purchased apartment. No apparent marriage plans on the horizon anywhere. I am sure Wendy is waiting anxiously for the arrival of dozens of grandchildren.

Both boys are rather private individuals, much like their father, whereas Natalie communicates every moment of every day. I must confess to leaving the dining table regularly while she was relating the day's events at her office.

Jason took up playing poker and had a surprising substantial win, which made him decide to follow this line of making a living. The early success has never been repeated and he has recently returned to a more mundane lifestyle with regular work and only occasional visits to the poker table.

8

A Liquidator's Perspective

When I left school in 1954, I had no idea what I wanted to do with my life. Securing a geological job in the gold mines satisfied my need to further educate myself as well as giving me some financial security. My move to Rhodesia in 1957 brought me to what I regarded as a paradise. My days in the field were filled with wonderful experiences. And then, I completely changed direction. How strange that I would eventually join a firm which was about to go bust and so set me on a road filled with interest and experiences the like of which I could never have imagined in my wildest dreams.

A liquidation order relates to companies, while insolvency deals with individuals. The effect of a liquidation order on a company is to immediately wrestle the powers of its directors from them and place the entire company's affairs in the hands of the appointed liquidator. The liquidator, once granted powers of sale by the courts, will endeavour to realise as much as possible from the existing assets and distribute the proceeds to the company's creditors. Certain creditors have preferential claims over some assets; e.g. mortgages on immovables; hire purchase agreements on other assets. Once all assets have been realised and are distributed, the company ceases to exist. There are interim measures that can be placed on companies; I refer to judicial managements and administration orders.

The purpose of such orders is to provide the administrators time to investigate the company's affairs and, if possible, to put the company back on its feet. Should there be no grounds for keeping the company going, it will then be placed in liquidation.

Where an individual is declared insolvent, his estate vests in the hands of an appointed trustee. He no longer has control of his finances; his assets are realised for the benefit of his creditors and his/her affairs remain with the trustee, until such time as the insolvent obtains his/her rehabilitation. Only then is he permitted to accumulate 'wealth'. The laws governing these legal proceedings vary from country to country. They do, however, serve the same purpose. Usually, rehabilitation of an individual will not be granted during a period of less than two years. Naturally, should all creditors be paid in full, an earlier application for rehabilitation can be made and will usually succeed.

A liquidator's role is not necessarily a destructive one. Quite often it is advantageous to keep the business operating, while assessing the reasons for its collapse. Manufacturing concerns invariably have work in progress and it is obviously more financially beneficial to creditors to sell off finished goods than to close operations promptly and realise virtually nothing for unfinished items still on the work benches.

Zimbabwe has a climate that is conducive to growing many different crops. Again, I found it better to bring some crops to fruition. Tobacco has always been the country's prime crop. As this has a specific growing period, I tried to get the crop to market, even though this may take many weeks to accomplish.

The weather, too, plays its part. Drought can have a devastating effect on the quantity and quality of the crops in the ground. During my time, I have been involved in liquidating farming operations ranging from over thirty different crops.

Tobacco is the most complicated, while maize is the least. More interesting are crops like coffee, tea, wheat and cotton to name a few of the larger scale operations. I also liquidated one of the biggest tomato and onion farms in Africa. What an interesting experience. Did you know that onions grow in 'sets'?

Perhaps, for me, the most interesting aspect of my job was determining the reasons for a business's collapse. In Zimbabwe, the cause usually centred around the economy and politics. I always enjoyed a good 'whodunit'. Believe me, I found plenty.

A jersey manufacturing company was placed into liquidation. In the factory, I found high up on the shelves many large boxes. Most of these had old rags hanging out of them. On investigation, I discovered that literally hundreds of new jerseys had been hidden. The workforce had placed the jerseys there out of sight and whenever the opportunity arose, they would remove a few to take back to their homes for selling to their families and friends. You will not be surprised to learn that the value of the stock I found in those boxes would have saved the company from closure. Unfortunately, in a liquidation, the realisation of such bulk does not fetch the true value of the goods.

Livestock liquidations have also been varied. Apart from cattle, pigs and sheep, I have also been involved with ostriches and crocodiles. I discovered that every single ounce of an ostrich can be put to a commercial use. Even its feet are used for umbrella and walking stick handles.

It has been on the commercial operations that I came across most cases of fraud. Only a few could be attributed to a lack of managerial skills. Perhaps the most unusual was the funeral parlours I had to keep going until all the corpses had been claimed and buried. I have selected some of these which I consider will be of interest to the reader and highlight just how much I have enjoyed my working life.

Piet

My initial opinion of the roll of a liquidator was one of depression, destruction and general negativity; lacking in purpose and job satisfaction. This was a result of the liquidation of the Supreme Holdings group in 1974. How wrong I was.

In 1975 I had my first appointment after Supreme, in an insolvency case involving a maize farmer, Piet, as he was known. He got the familiar itch which happens to men at the age of 40. He dumped his wife and married a pretty young miss with expensive tastes. Before long he found himself on the wrong side of his creditors. He started moving his crop of maize to the farm of his new mother-in-law in the middle of the night.

His movements were spotted by a neighbouring farmer, (John Cinamon), who notified the police. Piet was arrested on the suspicion of attempting to defraud his creditors. During my investigation into his affairs I noted that he had purchased 6000 unused maize bags from the Farmers' Co-op. He had only pooled 1300 full bags of maize at the local maize depot. When I asked him what had become of the balance of 4700 empty bags, he had no answer and owned up to the fraud. Simple arithmetic! I am, after all, an accountant. I have not related this matter to blow my own trumpet however. During my interrogations in court of Piet, his mother-in-law, and his wife, I questioned his wife on a particularly large diamond engagement ring on her finger. I was hoping to have the purchase of the ring set aside, which I am permitted to do under insolvency law in Rhodesia should I find the funds for the purchase came from Piet. I must mention that I had requested a police presence in court to have Piet formally charged once I had been able to extract an admission of guilt from him.

His wife's answer to my question was met with a stunned silence by all in the courtroom as she related how her husband had met some 'travellers' from South Africa. These men had prevailed upon Piet to sell, on their behalf, two large diamonds for which he would be rewarded with a third one for his efforts. Hence the engagement ring. I had done my bit and the police took over. I found out later from a friend of mine in the police that they had sprung a trap for the smugglers with Piet's assistance. A sophisticated smuggling operation was accordingly brought to a dramatic end. As for Piet, he got a suspended sentence due his assistance and with the fact that his mother-in-law agreed to pay his creditors in full.

Reg

Reg was a farmer; a big farmer. Big in size and big in the size of his farming operations. His cotton farm in the Bindura district was one of the more prosperous in Zimbabwe. He was married and had two sons who were in their early teens when I became involved in Reg's life. I found him a very jolly person, full of fun and good humour.

At the age of 40 Reg got the 'itch'. I refer to that sexual phenomenon of casting a wild eye in the direction of every pretty young miss in the hope of finding a path into her bed. Reg's prey was a nineteen year old blonde. He became completely besotted. So much so that he neglected his family, his farm and his friends. His wife was not prepared to give up without a fight and followed Reg whenever he left the farm in the hope of confronting him and his amour.

Reg told me of the many narrow escapes he had; ducking under bushes; hiding in supermarkets and driving off into the wilderness to mention but a few. His favourite hiding place was on Kariba dam. Here he and his young lover could go off on a boat for days. His wife usually spotted his car but was not able to devote too much time waiting for the couple to return. On one occasion, she did collar him alone but was informed that he had gone fishing 'with the boys.' Inevitably the truth came out and Reg found himself divorced and insolvent. I was appointed liquidator of his farming company and trustee of his estate. I sold off the assets and finalized the estates. The story does not end there.

The young lady now had Reg to herself and started marriage plans. I am not sure if she was aware that her lover had lost all his wealth. In the meantime, Reg was having second thoughts. Things had progressed and he was now an engaged man. His intended set the date. And Reg now got cold feet!

The day before the wedding was to take place, he persuaded a policeman friend of his to lock him up in jail. He contacted his bride minutes before the ceremony informing her that he could not make the wedding as he was in jail. She was waiting with her parents at the registry office. She was beside herself with fury and called Reg every name under the sun.

She was not to be deterred and set another date two weeks later. As you might expect, our hero tried the same trick again. Two hours later, while he was languishing in the prison cell, his bride stormed in with a Justice of the Peace and her parents in tow. They were married there and then.

I lost touch with events for a while. I had taken up golf and, one day about three years later, met Reg's ex-wife on a golf course in Harare. We had a drink after the game and I enquired after Reg. She told me that he had once again been divorced. She then went on to tell me that a few months earlier, Reg had come knocking on her door in a very sorry state. He told her he was hungry and asked her if she could see her way to giving him a meal. As Reg had obviously not washed in some time she told him to take a bath while she prepared some food for him. When the meal was ready she knocked on the bathroom door. There was no response so she opened the door and found Reg dead in the bath. He had died of a heart attack.

Jane

Jane was unfortunate to be married to someone who spent all her money and once the coffers were empty, ran off to find another sucker. They had a joint bank account for which Jane had stood as guarantor. The bank obviously looked to Jane to make good the deficit. This was not a huge amount by normal standards but as Jane had no means of paying off the debt she applied for an insolvency order thereby avoiding civil imprisonment. When Jane came to me as her trustee, she was completely destitute and was only surviving through the kindness of a few friends.

She asked me if I could lend her a small amount of money until she could find a job. She was living in a small country village at the time and job prospects were bleak. I asked her if there was anything else she could do. She informed me of a hobby of hers making African dolls out of a compound called Trinepon. I asked her if I might see one which she produced the next day. These dolls were about 18 inches in height. The doll's clothing comprised of the leaves covering a maize cob. These were painted with colours extracted from roots and fruit; all in all, very attractive.

Apart from the cost of the compound her expenses were minimal. I agreed to advance her sufficient to buy enough Trinepon for ten dolls to test the market plus a little extra for her personal upkeep. The rest is history.

My loan was repaid in a matter of weeks. Jane's creditors were paid in full within a couple of years. She was duly rehabilitated. I did learn from her that her now ex-husband had landed his next prey in a similar deep hole. My only reason for relating this is because it showed me what can be done where there is a will and a little luck.

This early experience in my career as a liquidator gave me the realisation that I was in a position to help persons in deserving cases, and over the next twenty odd years I was able to assist many people who through bad luck had found themselves in difficult financial circumstances. I shan't claim to have experienced a completely successful record as I fell prey to con artists on a couple of occasions. This did not diminish my willingness to assist where I felt reasonably comfortable.

I was appointed liquidator in the matter of a large motor spare parts company. This company had outlets in several cities, the largest being in Bulawayo. And it was from this city I received an offer from an emergent businessman for a job lot. The amount involved was Z$750000, a very respectable sum considering the country's plight. This included the company's other assets as well as the stock. The purchaser requested a brief period in which to pay. After securing a deposit, I agreed. A month later, I had not received any more money. I travelled to Bulawayo to confront the purchaser. He met me with a huge smile on his face asking for a little more time to settle. I had no option but to agree.

A month later and still no money. Another visit to Bulawayo. When I arrived at the company's premises I was shocked to find them empty. I managed to catch up with the buyer who informed me that he had sold all the assets and was waiting for his money. I demanded to meet the new buyer and was informed that the assets had been sold to a company controlled by my buyer. He had outwitted me. So much for my trusting everyone until they crossed me!

To cut a long story short, I took the matter to court and lost my case. It had all taken many months. There was a small compromise in that the buyer claimed to have bought the assets on consignment to his company and thereby, I, as liquidator, was still the legal owner. I was able to recover what remaining assets I could locate. On auction, I realised under $50000. There was no point in seeking further legal redress. I had been 'taken to the cleaners'.

I did on one occasion stick my neck out for a much larger sum. I was appointed liquidator of a dam construction company. It was obvious from the outset that there was no possibility of completing the project. Due to the specialised nature of the company's equipment, I could not see that an auction sale would have any public interest. The value of the equipment ran to several million dollars. There were some young men who had been employed on the dam. They approached me to lease/buy the equipment. Their plan was to construct small dams for farms with the equipment acquired from my 'loan' to them. It took more than five years to make good the loan together with interest. My sleepless nights were also of a substantial number. These men were still in business when I retired.

Leo

Due to the changing political scene and the difficult financial climate, an acquaintance of mine, named Leo, did an overnight flit from Zimbabwe and settled in Cyprus. Leo and I had had business dealings in the past and I was aware of some of his shady dealings. As luck would have it, I was appointed trustee of his estate which was sequestrated once it became apparent he had done a runner.

I soon found out he had moved his valuables to the home of his young teenage daughter. As one would expect, she claimed the numerous assets were her property and not her father's. I found it highly unlikely that this youngster could have amassed such wealth and proceeded to attach the assets for the benefit of Leo's creditors. I had to warn her of the seriousness of her situation and that she could face imprisonment if she tried to hide or dispose of any asset not her property. Naturally, she contacted her father who in turn contacted me in a very threatening manner. Having had dealings with Leo in the past, I told him to stop being an idiot and for the sake of his daughter, accept that I would deal with her fairly and sympathetically.

In due course, once I received powers of sale I sent Leo's assets to the auctioneers for sale. All but two paintings were sold. Try as he might the auctioneer could not get any bids for these paintings. I wanted to finalise the estate and pay the proceeds to creditors. I instructed the auctioneer to find any buyer even himself if necessary and I would then take over the paintings and compensate him for his cash input.

I was delighted to learn he had personally bought the two paintings for Z$600. (This was his reliable valuation.) At the time that would have amounted to about £500 sterling. The one painting was very dark; the other, very modern and not my taste. I gave the modern painting to the auctioneer for his troubles and paid him his Z$600. Two weeks later I received a cheque from the auctioneer advising me he had sold the modern painting for Z$600 and the cheque was for the proceeds less his normal fee. I now had a painting which had cost me, more or less, nothing.

I took the painting to South Africa when I married Wendy. She wanted to know more about it and took it to the Johannesburg Art Gallery. They cleaned it up and reframed it. We learnt the painting was the work of a 19th century German artist named Heindrich Ewers. I still have the painting in our lounge.

One last thing to mention. At a dinner of an art enthusiast, I related how I came to be in possession of my painting. He had a CD with details of sales of 650000 paintings sold in the last ten years. From this, he ascertained that recently, two works by Ewers had been sold on auction, both realising over £10000. My masterpiece is slightly damaged and I am sure it is not worth such a handsome amount. Perhaps one day I will summon up the courage to have it valued. For the time being I am quite happy to dream on and avoid disappointment.

Pete

Pete Smith was another person to leave the country in a hurry. He was a tobacco buyer on the auction floors. Pressure from his American masters caused Pete to make some poor judgement calls. He also started speculating on a variety of avenues to increase his wealth for his growing family. He left the country before anyone realised he was gone. Just up and went with his wife, two young children and very little else. The problem arose from a huge hole in his employers' finances. My appointment as his trustee necessitated my tracking down the missing funds. His house was situated in a prime suburb and its contents were all top of the range. However, the total value of his visible assets did not even amount to 5% of the shortfall. During my investigation, I got the impression that here was a man caught up in a situation not of his making. It seemed he had no alternative other than to flee as he was facing a certain prison term had he remained.

I managed to track Pete to London and booked myself on an airplane. When I finally had Pete agree to a meeting, it was only in the presence of his lawyer at that law firm's office. The meeting was a complete washout as his lawyer advised him not to answer even one of the many questions I put to him. Realising I was wasting my time I departed. I had organised a taxi to stand by to collect me after the meeting. As I approached the taxi, I discovered I had left my raincoat at the reception. I collected my coat and I decided to have a comfort break while I was able. Guess who I met in the toilet?

Pete took me to an unoccupied office and willingly gave satisfactory answers to most of my queries. His lawyer would have killed him had she realised what had happened. Life is certainly very strange.

On that same trip, I also managed to track down a television celebrity chef who had left the country owing more than he could hope to repay. I found him running a pub in New Alford. I arrived at the pub unannounced. He could not believe I had hunted him down. He agreed to send monthly amounts to Zimbabwe for the benefit of his creditors. His indebtedness was not large and there seemed little point in giving him a hard time as he was prepared to co-operate.

And I was lucky to find yet another insolvent, an elderly man, living in Chester. The visit to that stunning town was worth the visit even if I was not able to extract any funds from the man. I was greeted at his front door by the man's wife who asked me what business I had with her husband. It transpired she was completely unaware her husband had left Zimbabwe owing quite a fair amount. It turned out that she held the purse strings and offered to pay half the debt. This seemed the best result from my point of view and I agreed.

All in all, a very satisfactory trip.

Dan

While I was on one of my army duties I was put in charge of a 'stick' of six other men. One of them was a man named Brian. This man was, in my humble opinion, a shirker. Almost every time we went out on patrol Brian had an upset stomach and disappeared in the direction of the latrines.

Brian was also an accountant, practicing with a large professional firm. In the mid-1980s he took up an appointment as liquidator of a fair-sized trading company in the Karoi district of Zimbabwe. This company, with a few others, was owned by a certain Dan. Brian immediately set about attempting to take control of the other enterprises as well as petitioning the courts for Dan's estate to be sequestrated and for he, Brian, to be appointed in all these matters.

One morning, I found Dan waiting in my offices. He came

to request that I oppose Brian's petitions, on the grounds that he was not insolvent, nor were his companies. One thing you learn as an accountant is how to manipulate figures on balance sheets to suit your purposes. This is a time worn practice and one in which I was sure Brian was as adept as anyone. I can't be sure that I was not motivated by a desire to clash with Brian, a person I really did not like. The only way to get to the truth was to be given enough time. As the return day for confirmation of Brian's applications was fast approaching, I had to act quickly. I petitioned for an urgent judicial management order over Dan's estate and all other companies to which Brian had not yet been appointed. The courts were presented with a financial dilemma and fortunately looked favourably on the judicial management application as an interim measure. Brian went ballistic.

And so, the battle commenced. We churned out figures and more figures, and even more figures. I was gradually able to see some sunlight through the trees and started to believe in Dan's assertions. Insolvency hearings are held before The Master of the High Court. Proceedings were fairly even until Brian virtually called me a liar claiming the figures I had produced before the courts were a complete fabrication of the real state of Dan's affairs. The Master took exception to this on my behalf and made Brian openly and unreservedly apologize.

Shortly thereafter, my application for judicial management order was granted. Then all I had to do was prove my case which meant being able to pay off Dan's creditors. In time, this was achieved and the judicial order on Dan and his companies was lifted. I had been vindicated much to my relief. My relations with Brian never improved. He took on the role of liquidator in more cases but our paths seldom crossed.

A couple of years later I took Brenda to a very smart newly established dining venue. I don't remember what we were celebrating; we had so much to be thankful for. The venue was amazing, the food stunning and the champagne flowed freely. The service was excellent apart from when I asked to settle the bill. I must have asked about four times and it was only when I was losing my patience that the maitre d' brought me a compliments slip. It read: 'Dinner is on me. Thanks for everything. Best wishes; Dan.'

I found out shortly after that Dan and his wife had recently opened the restaurant. The next occasion we went there, the same thing happened. What a pity! I had to find another place to dine.

Guardian Trust undertook secretarial and accounting responsibilities as well as the normal trust duties associated with a trust company. On the day that Woods did not return to the office, an important farming client had made an appointment. The Millers became very agitated at the delay. The staff had no idea why Woods had not come to work as his body had yet to be discovered. Apart from offering profuse apologies and umpteen cups of tea there was little we could do. Mrs Miller threatened to take their business elsewhere and only relented when I promised that someone would come to their farm the next day.

I did visit them as promised and had to inform them of Woods' death. I managed to persuade them not to take their business away and informed them that I was a qualified accountant and would be able to attend to their needs and ensure that their tax problems would be handled in a manner that would legally benefit them and not the Collector of Taxes. (Woods, due to his strict discipline, expected everyone to pay their full dues.)

This started my business dealings with two of the nicest people I have ever had the privilege of serving. Their farming activities were vast and diverse. They had come from Lancashire and their dealings with the labourers on the farm were always fair and sympathetic. When the political problems started on the farms, I felt the Millers had done more than enough to ensure their labourers would vouch for them as having always had the interests and welfare of everyone on the farm at heart. That is why I found it so difficult to understand why Mr. Miller was slaughtered by his work force and Mrs Miller and her daughter were given two hours to vacate the farm.

Lock Ups

One of my early liquidations involved a bus company. The company owned many buses, most of which were nonrunners at the time of the liquidation. In fact, everything was in a sad, sad state. The law gives secured creditors preference in these matters if they can positively identify their security. Accordingly, I contacted the five hire purchase companies in Salisbury to meet me at the bus company's premises at ten o'clock on the morning of the placement of the bus company under my control. The premises were vast whereas the office of the business was no bigger than a normal sized bedroom. Needless to say, the telephone company had suspended phone services many months earlier.

The representatives of the finance companies and I gathered in the office and I explained to them what I expected of them, for them to secure their claim. We then headed for the door of the office to venture into the grounds to inspect engine numbers and other identifiable items. There was however, a major problem. I am not referring to the messy state of the assets.

The workers had locked us in the office! I tried communicating with the workers' spokesman through the only window which was heavily barred. I failed completely. The men locked up with me were not impressed to say the least. We were not even allowed the comfort of a toilet break and were told to use the waste paper basket. We did manage to get a few mugs of water from them. Obviously, we could not drink too much water due to our lack of toilet facilities. And so, the day dragged on as my companions got more fed up by the minute.

In Africa, night falls very quickly. One minute it is still light and suddenly it is pitch black. Of course, the electricity supply had been cut some time back. In the office, I had come to the decision that we would have to break out through the roof once the workers had gone home for the night. This presumed that they would not leave some form of guard. Then just before sunset, common sense prevailed and we were told we could go home. My earlier talks through the window with some of the workers had given them something to chew on regarding their rights and future prospects. At the time of the liquidation they had already reached the point where they had nothing ahead of them and the liquidation proved to be a timely intervention in their lives.

I can't say anyone was happy to be freed but at least we were unharmed and not too much the worse for our ordeal.

I was 'locked up' on another five occasions. The second involved a very big clothing factory. I had foolishly climbed up onto a gantry high above the factory floor. From there, I could address the several hundred workers and inform them of my plans to close the company but not before all work in progress had been completed. This would afford the workers of a little more pay and give them time to look for other work. It would also prove beneficial to the company's creditors. You guessed it. I spent the rest of the day up there. Towards evening I was asked to sign a scrap of paper stating I promised to return the next day. That was it. Everybody was happy and we all went home.

Another liquidation was not such a happy affair. This was the matter of a suitcase manufacturing company. It is nearly always the case that by the time a liquidation order is made, the business is in a very sorry state. This company was no exception and all the assets, mainly industrial sewing machines, had been badly vandalized by the workforce. I had been warned that this group of workers was indeed a 'nasty bunch'. A judicial order for liquidation/insolvency is always made on a Wednesday. Having been warned, I contacted the auctioneers who I would appoint to sell the assets once I received powers of sale. (This is only given on the 'return day' thus giving interested parties time to oppose the liquidation should they have grounds for so doing.) I instructed them to remove all assets from the factory after the workers had left for the day.

The next morning, I entered the factory to inform the workers of the liquidation. As in most cases, there was no lighting or telephone service. Such services are usually disconnected if not paid promptly. I was confronted by an extremely hostile workforce, whose anger intensified due to the assets having been removed the previous evening. They managed to corner me in a very dark part of the factory. I must confess to having serious concerns for my safety. The noise level from the shouting mob was intense. So much so, that it attracted the attention of a security guard from the next factory.

What an incredibly brave man. He came up to me and whispered that I should stand close to him. He told me to stay alongside him as he literally walked us both out of the factory, all the time talking to the angry mob. We were both in the clear before the workers realised what had happened. I never found out his name and though I had thanked him profusely at the time, I felt it was not enough. I did communicate with his boss later and sent him a reward. I wish I could have done more.

The last time I was 'locked up' was in the matter of a jersey manufacturing company, one of the largest concerns of this nature in Africa. By this time, I was familiar with the pattern. I was fairly certain I would be held by the workers and was just as certain, come the end of the day, I would be free to go home to my wife, Brenda. She had recently given birth to our youngest boy. Sure enough, at the end of the day, I was approached by some people. I was sitting in a chair in a confined space in one of the factory's corners and noticed one of the persons held a TV camera and another a microphone as seen on news reports. I was informed they were from the BBC and they enquired what was happening. I was in no mood to be co-operative as I had been sitting in that chair for some eight hours. I simply told them I wanted to go home and asked them to get me out of there. I was told that they could not do so as they had only been granted permission to interview me on the understanding that they did not interfere in any way whatsoever.

What I did not know was that my wife, Brenda, was sitting at home breastfeeding our new baby watching the television. She saw her husband being interviewed by the BBC, locked up by workers in a factory somewhere in Harare. All's well that ends well. Come evening I was released and went home into the welcoming arms of my tearful wife.

A liquidator's role is not always destructive. Though not frequent, there are occasions where there is a successful outcome. One such instance involved a gold mine called Stori's Golden Shaft. During my geological career, I was part of the team conducting an evaluation of the mine for Anglo American. The conclusion reached at the time found that the property was too small to interest a large mining house like Anglo.

In the early 1990s an acquaintance of mine had obtained the right to conduct mining operations at Stori's. He spent a great deal of money exploring for gold at depth. When his funds ran out, I was appointed Judicial Manager. My recollection of earlier investigations with Anglo concluded that the gold bearing veins were lenticular and pinched out with depth. I also recalled that we had found several parallel gold bearing veins near the surface.

I gave instructions to carry out horizontal borehole drilling from one of the mine's drives. The rest is history. An ore body was intersected and, once mined, produced more gold in a couple of months than during the entire mining period of the previous five years. Everyone was paid in full and the mine was still producing some ten years later. I was given a lump of gold bearing quartz the size of a brick as a souvenir which I use as a paperweight on my desk to this day. The amount of visible gold in this rock is incredible.

I find it quite remarkable how the different career paths I chose have converged to benefit and assist my work loads. I suppose this endorses my fatalistic philosophy. The same can be said about people and friends. I don't think it is a good idea to let work combine with friendship. Yet in my business role I have been able to assist some of my best friends to overcome business problems and still maintain a close friendship base.

One particular matter was in the case of Scottish Jewellers. This company had been run successfully, for many years, by a good friend of mine named Allan. I met Allan when I joined Round Table, a young men's service organisation which apart from doing good works for charity, also was a platform from which many of my lasting friendships were founded. Enter Allan. He along with four other Tablelers made up our weekly bridge sessions. There were many other social get-togethers including Scottish country dancing. As can be expected, not everybody got along. At one of the dancing sessions a chap, who shall remain nameless, deliberately tripped another friend of mine. The subsequent fallout was predictable and that ended our, and several others' enjoyment of 'stripping the willow'.

Allan owned Scottish Jewellers and, as far as I knew, ran it very successfully. With the passing of years and the deterioration of Rhodesia's economy Scottish Jewellers was put into liquidation. I was appointed and had to investigate the company's activities. This proved to be a highly delicate task, but I am pleased to say my friendship with Allan survived right up to the day he died many years later. We celebrated a Christmas lunch at Allan's house at Margate in Natal. He had opened a new

Scottish Jewellers and had remarried an American lass, Kay, who prepared an American style Christmas lunch. The amount of food put on the table was amazing. Regrettably the amount of food consumed did not do Kay's efforts justice. Every dish had a certain 'sweetness' about it; probably maple syrup; definitely not to my, nor to most of the other guests', taste.

Kay still runs the jewellers and we keep in touch. I hope one day to visit her; but definitely not for Christmas lunch!

On several occasions I had to exercise judicial functions which had political undertones. Needless to say, I had to tread carefully whenever I became so involved.

In 1983, Mugabe banned Nkomo's ZAPU. I was appointed either liquidator (companies) or trustee (individuals and businesses not formed into companies) in all of ZAPU's activities. These were numerous and situated throughout the country. The largest by far was Nijo, a tomato and onion growing business. This was probably the jewel in the crown in Nkomo's assets. It was apparent from the start that Mugabe had his eye on this acquisition. Its liquidation did succeed in bringing order to the situation. All creditors were paid in full. The only loser was Nkomo. From then until he died, I had a long association with this giant of a man not only as the 'father' of a nation, but also in his physical stature. I had to purchase an especially large chair for him to sit on when he visited my offices.

I suppose we could have become friends had it not been for his part in ordering the downing of two Viscount aircraft thereby killing many innocent civilians. Notwithstanding, our relationship was always cordial. He always referred to me as 'My dear'. His main focus was the return of the properties Mugabe had taken from him. Of course, this was never going to happen.

Early one morning, I was summoned to a meeting at his residence. I arrived at the requested time of 7.00 a.m. His housekeeper brought me refreshments and went to wake the great man. When he appeared at 7.45, I had extreme difficulty not to burst out laughing as he was attired in a floor-length night gown and had a nightcap on his head. After our meeting, I walked to my vehicle which was a brand new VW Caravelle. So new, in fact, that it was making a lot of ticking noises due to the expansion of metal from the heat generated while driving to the meeting. Imagine my horror when I found six heavily armed soldiers prowling round the van in their belief that a time bomb was about to go off. I was arrested there and then and only released some forty minutes later after Nkomo had completed his morning ablutions. He informed them I was not trying to kill them all.

One of my more scary appointments occurred as liquidator of a company owned by a South African business man. He had invested substantial sums in developing a holiday site on Lake Kyle. The company had constructed double storey holiday chalets of a very unique design and the potential for the sight was enormous. The Minister of Home Affairs had seen the project and wanted it for himself. He declared the South African a prohibited person and placed his own minions on the site, barring access to all and sundry. The minister, Mubaka, had overlooked the fact that some large creditors were seeking payment. He unsuccessfully opposed the liquidation order and I was appointed. I shall not go into details of the political pressure and instructions I received to keep out of Mubaka's business. Suffice to say, it became necessary for me to report the interference to the Justice Minister, who carried a bigger stick in Mugabe's government. Problem solved, though not without more threats. (The Justice Minister is today Zimbabwe's vice president.)

One other political appointment was in the matter of a car dealer and his wife named Paweni. Both were incarcerated on corruption charges. In 1984 Paweni was awarded a huge contract to transport maize for drought food throughout the country.

He was accused of bribing senior government officials, even ministers, by getting them to accept false invoices for which he was paid by the Zimbabwe treasury. Paweni had opened car dealerships throughout the country. The majority of cars were imported and the obvious question arose; where did he get the money to finance such a large operation? These cars were passed on as reward to those officials who had given assistance to Paweni.

My function was to ascertain proof of corruption and to what extent this involved other persons in high up places. As my normal work load was already hectic at the time, I obtained assistance from a couple of accountants, who were in a position to devote 16 hours a day to the task. We set to work and completed the undertaking in a few weeks. Our plan was to track the destination of each and every vehicle that came into Paweni's business. Once again, I shall refrain from going into all the details. The report I tabled was comprehensive and thorough. In all over thirty persons were found to have been involved, ranging from senior government secretaries to police officers.

To the best of my knowledge, not one other person was held to account let alone dismissed. Paweni died in prison. His wife served several years behind bars.

I feel I must make one last reference to the political aspect of my many years doing work on behalf of the government. In not one single instance did I find Mugabe even remotely connected to corruption or commercial wrongdoing. Of course, I exclude his acquisition of Nkomo's assets, where all creditors were settled in full.

There is one last curious happening I wish to relate. Once again, my chosen paths of employment interacted. While I was working for Anglo American, a newly qualified geologist from England, joined the Anglo team. Ken came from very a humble background where his family had very little money. Suddenly

Ken found he had plenty as his job was well paid. Unfortunately, Ken saw fit 'to flash the cash' He took to treating everyone in the local pub, where he was stationed, to endless rounds of drinks. He, too, started consuming more than was good for him.

Although I was some years younger than Ken, I was asked to 'straighten him out'. We were sent to investigate a small gold mine (Roof Mine), which was situated in a remote area in the north of Rhodesia. There was not a pub within thirty miles of Roof, and my instructions included a 'no alcohol' camp.

I thought the plan to keep Ken 'dry' was going well for a while. But then, things changed. Ken had managed to get a local man to buy his booze for him and hid his acquisitions underground in the mine's workings. I stumbled on cases and cases of beer quite by chance when taking samples of the reef. I got my gang of helpers to move the cases to a different underground sight and to seal off the cavern with large rocks and rubble. Ken was furious when he could not find his supplies.

He did not speak to me for nearly a month, by which time we were moved to another project. And Ken was sober and more co-operative. We left Roof Mine and the beer behind. Anglo decided the mine had no further interest to them. There had been good results from our samples but as the ore body contained arsenic sulphide, extraction of the gold would always prove difficult.

Many years later, I was appointed trustee of an insolvent who had been conducting mining operations at Roof Mine. (How strange is that?) I had met the insolvent some time back and as he too was a geologist, I had suggested to him to have a look at Roof.

On arriving at the mine, one of the first things I did was to go in search of the hidden beer. With the aid of some underground mapping I found the sight. As far as I could see, it had not been touched and the insolvent confirmed that his activities had been confined to a different part of the mine.

Some hours later the rocks and rubble had been removed and there in front of my eyes was the cache of beer. Or so I thought. Not so. Every case was there and every bottle was in its case. Every bottle had been opened and the contents drained or should I say drunk!

Just another of my life's mysteries.

I estimate that during my time at Guardian Trust, I must have been involved in nearly 800 different matters. Most were routine but nearly every matter had some facet to it that held my interest. I count myself fortunate to have lived most of my working life in an occupation with so little routine and with so much variety.

9

Animals, Fish And Insects

I must confess to not being the best of carers of my pets. I do not excuse myself and put this failing down to my childhood. Being at boarding school, we never had pets at home. This did not diminish my desire to have pets; it just did not provide me with the best background on how to care for them. There are a couple of incidents that I wish to relate.

In 1957, my first location with Anglo American was on the Sabi River. I and another geologist named Bob were investigating a phosphate deposit. Our team of labourers were cutting a line through the bush for mapping purposes. I got the fright of my life when something sprang out of a tree as it was falling, ran up my trouser leg and dived into my trouser pocket. Needless to say I whipped down my trousers and kept the intruder secured in the pocket. I was informed that I had trapped a squirrel.

Our camp comprised a tent for sleeping and a very smart pole and mud office/ dining area, the roof of which was covered with palm leaves. It was a magical site right on the banks of the river next to a fair sized pool where we regularly caught fish for our meals.

I managed to extricate the squirrel from my pocket and placed it in a cardboard box. Over the next three days all my attempts to give the squirrel food and water failed. On the fourth morning while eating my cereal with long life milk, I decided to release the squirrel from captivity. I lifted the lid off the box, which was on the table next to my plate. I could not believe what happened next. After a couple of minutes the squirrel left the box, came up to my plate of cereal and started drinking and munching at my breakfast. Bob took a photo but regrettably I never kept a copy. We did not try to recapture the squirrel. But watched it climb up into our palm leaved roof.

You might expect that to be the end of the story. You would be wrong. The squirrel must have made a nest in the roof or whatever squirrels do and regularly came down onto our dining table for a meal. Bob had a wind-up gramophone on which we played records at night. One night our squirrel came down and climbed onto the record which was revolving at a very slow speed as it needed to be wound up again. It sat trying to stay on while the turntable went round and round. We laughed and laughed and laughed at this amazing site. Then Bob pushed the speed of the gramophone up to 78 rpm. The cad!

The squirrel went flying off and ran back up to its nest in the roof.

I still chuckle to myself when I recall the moment. I am sure there is a smile on my face as I write this.

When we settled in our first house in England we bought a Yorkie puppy. Lottie was everyone's darling. She was extremely intelligent and very cute. As the children were in school and Wendy was at work, it fell to me to give Lottie the exercise she needed. I too, was busy. Apart from playing golf three times a week I also undertook some part time work at the golf club. Our neighbours across our cul-de-sac, took to walking Lottie quite frequently. Did I mention that Lottie was very intelligent?

Whenever she heard our neighbours come home she would jump up onto the window sill and bark and bark to go for 'walkies'. It did not take her long before she started digging under our fence to go to find our friends. Of course, our neighbours were not always at home. This prompted Lottie to go exploring and she would wander round the neighbourhood. A kindly lady living in the area brought Lottie to our front door and, quite rightly, instructed me to take better care of our dog.

Lottie was having a fine time escaping from home and the kindly lady brought her home again. On the third occasion, she warned me that the next time would result on my being reported for negligence. Lottie could not have cared less. Finally, in one hour she escaped three times. I had resorted to placing large building blocks at every point of escape, in an effort to prevent her from doing so. All to no avail. She was now digging more than six inches under concrete. I was at my wits end. I had to make a decision.

Lottie went to an animal shelter at Blue Cross. My family have never forgiven me.

I have a couple of other 'dog' incidents to relate briefly. Brenda and I bought a Bouviere bitch puppy who we named Lucky. We both never realised how large this breed grew. Lucky and our two baby boys grew up together. We needed to have no fear for our children as Lucky allowed them to pull and tug at her endlessly without as much as a growl. The only aggression she showed was when she chomped Garfield, a most beautiful large ginger cat we inherited from some people who left the country. When Garfield first arrived, he watched Lucky with eagle eyes, but the first time he let his guard down, was the end.

Lucky's claim to fame came after I lost Brenda and was in the process of moving to South Africa. One of Brenda's girlfriends, Fiona, lived in a remote part of Harare. She was separated and had two small children. One night two intruders broke into her poorly protected home. I gather they had been surveying the house for some time as it seemed a soft target. They were not aware that Lucky had recently moved in and slept in the children's bedroom. Their mistake! Lucky literally floored both intruders and cornered them in the room until the police arrived to take them away. The front page of the Herald had a picture of Lucky the following day.

The other story relates to a Great Dane owned by Sarah, one of my senior staff at Guardian Trust. Shortly before leaving Africa I was invited to attend a farewell staff dinner at Sarah's home. I was placed at one end of the table, enjoying the company, the wine, and the dinner, when I became aware of this huge head near my ear. That is how large this dog was. Worse still, the dog was slobbering all over my jacket and longs and onto my plate.

I protested, perhaps too vigorously. Sarah did eventually call the 'beast' away.

Some while later when I had settled in England, I heard Sarah had also left Zimbabwe and was living in Kent. I did endeavour to get together socially but it has never happened. I guess it is because she brought her dog with her and I declined an invitation to visit her at her home (because of the dog).

Recently, our cat, Holly, started bringing live mice into our home. She would play with them until they gave up the ghost. Or worse still, they hid away where Holly could not get at them and there they would die. Eventually the stink in the house would alert me to the fact that we had to go on a 'treasure' hunt. In one week we found eight mice. Once again, I faced a crisis as we were about to go on holiday and the house would stand empty. Once again, I took the unpopular decision to get rid of my problem. I gave Holly to our son living some ten miles away. On the fourth day, at his flat, Holly saw an open door and ran.

We scoured the area for hours. I placed a photo of her in the nearby supermarket. Even Facebook had her details. I must have knocked on over two hundred doors asking if anyone had seen her.

Five weeks later we got a call. Holly had been found and identified through the chip we had had inserted when we first got her. She is safely home. I will not take the easy way out again.

I think she has forgiven me. I am not sure whether the rest of my family have.

Wendy and I like travelling to different spots on our anniversaries and at Easter time.

One Easter weekend we visited Wales. On route to our destination at Fishguard, we spent a night in a B&B in the village of Abergavenny. We had been informed that this B&B was the best in the area. Details of the place are irrelevant and I shan't bore you with those details. After an uncomfortable night, we went in to breakfast. The dining room was very busy, and all twenty odd tables were occupied. At either end of the room there was a large square 'box' covered by a blanket. Our landlord entered the dining room and proceeded to welcome his 'guests'. In the process, he boosted the merits of his fine establishment. From one of the covered 'boxes' we heard a very loud but low pitched "F**K OFF". The entire room burst out laughing. Only our host failed to enjoy the moment. He removed the covering from both cages to reveal two magnificent African Grey parrots. Perhaps he should have left the covers on as over the next twenty odd minutes the two parrots exchanged the foulest language ever. I wonder where they picked up such a dialogue. Couldn't possibly be the landlord, could it?

I am not sure whether I have mentioned that I enjoy fishing. I don't have too many fishy tales to relate but there is one I think is worthy of a mention. It happened when I was on military duty in Rhodesia. Many 'older soldiers' were called up for duty from time to time. On this occasion, I was stationed at the Kariba dam on the mighty Zambesi River. The Zambesi separates Rhodesia/Zimbabwe from Zambia and during the 1970s it gave insurgents a relatively easy crossing point. Kariba dam provided most of the electric power to Rhodesia. We were grouped into pairs to take eight hour stints guarding various strategic points of the dam.

I and another man, Trevor, were put together for a week to guard the tail racers (i.e. at the foot of the dam wall). I had brought some fishing tackle with me. When we arrived at our station we found an African man fishing for tigerfish. These fish are perhaps the best sporting fish in the world. Trevor had never been fishing in his life, but was keen to catch his first. I asked the fisherman if he would kindly lend his rod to my colleague.

So while Trevor attempted to catch his first, I proceeded some fifty yards downstream to try to catch some bream for our supper. I had no joy as the tiger fish kept chomping my nylon fishing line. It was not long before Trevor called to me to come and help him as he had a fish on the line. I shouted back to him to catch his own fish. He was insistent and said he desperately needed help. I had my hands full trying to sort out my tackle so told him to bring his rod down to me. You must remember that this was the mighty Zambesi, a swift flowing and quite noisy river.

All our shouting had attracted the attention of our African fisherman. An excited Trevor managed to get to me as did an even more excited African. It was now obvious that Trevor had a sizeable fish on his line. Next thing, the African jumped into the river up to his shoulders. He wrapped his arms around the fish and with Trevor's help the two hauled this huge tiger fish onto the bank. Did I say huge? It was enormous! Trevor was beside himself while our African friend was in tears with happiness. I happened to have a Swiss army knife with me and the three of us managed to roughly measure the length and the circumference of the tiger. Approximately 47 inches long and 39 inches round at the biggest part. Regrettably we were unable to weigh it.

Later, we established that this was one of the largest tiger fish ever landed, and certainly the largest caught in the past ten years. That night we cooked some of the fish having given most of it to our African friend. I fried the fish in our army issue billycan and swallowed it down with some very excellent French wine. Trevor has a photo of his momentous catch. Regrettably I lost my copy some time ago.

I had another fishing trip where I landed some big cob. This was at a seaside venue in the Transkei. Many of the other holiday makers were expert fishermen and all were generous in parting with tips on which bait to use and when was the best time to go fishing. During the week, I caught a few fair sized fish. On my last day of the holiday, I proceeded to the beach with my tackle. Many of the men were sitting enjoying a beer before lunch on the hotel patio. I was informed that I was wasting my time as the fish would not be biting.

And so it proved; for a time! Suddenly I was aware of a large tug on my line. In my excitement to land my catch I almost lost it. Someone on the patio must have been watching me through binoculars, as before long I was surrounded by eager fishermen. When I finally landed this whopper, everyone clapped and applauded me. What a moment!

I expect most people are wary of snakes and I am no exception. During my geological exploration days I experienced two very close calls. The first one involved a black mamba, one of the deadliest snakes on earth. Its venom is lethal, usually within half an hour. I was oblivious to how close I came to death on this occasion. It was only a little later I realised how lucky I had been.

I had climbed into a pit to access a gold bearing reef for sampling purposes. At the bottom of the pit I had to crawl through a narrow tunnel to get my sample. Once achieved, I retreated and started to climb out of the pit. I looked up at the ashen face of my African assistant. He and another jumped into the pit and bodily lifted me out. Not knowing what it was all about, I was ready to give them both an earful. Within seconds of being out of the pit an enormous black mamba struck at me. Fortunate for me, its fangs only sank into my khaki longs. As we were many miles from any hospital I am positive I would not be relating this tale today had its fangs sunk into my leg.

The other snake that has caused me sleepless nights was a King Cobra. This reptile, while not as deadly as the mamba, can deliver a fatal venomous bite. On this occasion, I was driving along a very narrow track in the Zambesi valley. I saw this large cobra rise up in the middle of the track, only some dozen yards in front of me. Cobras, by nature, do not seek confrontation as a rule. But they are also known to be extremely aggressive.

I blasted the Land Rover's horn in an attempt to frighten it away. Nothing doing! If anything, I felt the cobra became even more hostile. The terrain did not permit me to put my vehicle in reverse. After a number of minutes with no sign of a backdown by the cobra I decided I would reluctantly have to shoot it. I am a reasonably good shot with my .303 rifle. I am positive the first shot hit the target. The cobra maintained its position in the middle of the track. In all, I fired seven more rounds into the snake. It finally collapsed, and I was able to slowly proceed back to camp. It must have taken me the best part of an hour. As I climbed out of the Land Rover, I felt a strike on my right boot. It was the cobra. Once again I was lucky it did not bite me higher up my leg. When driving over the cobra, it must have coiled itself to an underpart of the vehicle and hung on until we were motionless. Utterly amazing!

When Nick, my son, was fourteen I took him on a canoe safari on the mighty Zambesi. Our expedition started at Chirundu and there were six canoes in all including the one for our guide. I was many years older than the other people. What impressed me was the knowledge the younger persons had of the many trees along the banks of the river. We spent our first night sleeping under the stars on a small island in the river as our guide informed us there were many lions in the area and the island was the only safe place. I slept soundly and woke with the sun the next morning noticing an unpleasant smell nearby.

In fact, it was very near! Some two yards from my pillow was a huge heap of elephant's fresh dung. The whole area was full of recent elephant spoor and droppings. Our guide advised that they must have swum over to investigate while we were all asleep. No damage done. We moved on.

Our next excitement came a day later. Our guide informed us that if we saw hippos we had to ensure we did not block their path to deep water. We came across a number of hippos sunning themselves on a sandy bank and spent some time watching them as we circled round and round not to be swept downstream by the current. What nobody noticed was a lone bull hippo swimming in the deep water near our canoes. When he made his presence known he nearly overturned our guide's canoe. Only his experience saved him. I hate to think what the result might have been if the hippo had surfaced by my canoe.

The last two days were uneventful and two land rovers collected us at Mana Pools to return us to our starting point. Life is not always that simple. Our Land Rover broke down in the area frequented by lions. The front vehicle was not aware that we had stopped and continued its journey. It was many hours later that it returned during the gathering dusk. By the time we got going again it was pitch dark and the lions were roaring all around us. One even came close enough for a photo to be taken. This photo appeared in the newspaper a few days later.

I did experience hippo problems before this outing. I and another geologist had to investigate some radio-active anomalies in the Zambesi valley in 1958. We decided to set up camp close to the river. Camp consisted of a tent for sleeping and an adjacent flimsy structure of sticks and palm leaves where we were to have our meals and write our daily reports. When we arose after our first night, we found our stick structure flattened. No problem, we gave instructions to our helpers to resurrect it. The next morning, exactly the same thing. And same again the day after.

It was only towards evening on that third day that a wizened old man informed our helpers that we were erecting our shelter on the very path the hippos used to go foraging at night. We had not heard a thing. Just as well we had not erected our tent on that spot. We hastily moved our campsite; no more trouble.

My wife, Alison, was a beekeeper. Bees must rank as one of the most interesting creatures of our planet. We had three hives in the garden at home and I quickly learnt how to make myself useful. I was equipped with all the necessary clothing and head cover. Before long my confidence soared. And as you might suspect, I became more relaxed. One day I could not find my army boots and put on a pair of trainers not realising that the bees could get through the laces. That is exactly what happened and they started climbing up my legs inside my overalls.

The African bee is very much more aggressive than the European variety and their sting is that much greater. It was not long before I felt the first sting and then the second. With all the bees buzzing around, I could not start removing my clothing. Within minutes, I felt more stings on both legs. My solution was to wade in the water in our swimming pool, boots and all. Big mistake! This simply drove the bees further and further up my legs. I won't tell you how high they managed to get.

If you are a beekeeper, there is nothing more devastating than watching your bees being attacked by a swarm or robber bees. The latter swoop in, kill thousands of your bees including the queen bee and take your honey. Even more devastating but a thousand times more spectacular, is to witness your hive being bombarded by cardinal bee-eaters. These beautifully coloured birds act like a squadron of Spitfires and are just as deadly.

I have mentioned earlier visiting the racecourse. I love looking at horses and love watching them run even more. In my younger single days, I would set a budget for my gambling. Once that was blown I enjoyed the rest of the meeting just watching. In

Harare there were many, many rumours regarding which horse would win the next race. Quite often, my funds were depleted after the first race.

At one time, a couple of friends and I, started a pools company on horse racing, called Jabula Jackpots. After the initial early success, we made little progress. We were lucky enough to attract the displeasure of our largest competitor and were bought out. As I recall we barely covered our capital outlay.

Soon after this, a friend of mine was approached by a bookie for a substantial loan. Keith, the bookie, had got himself into big financial problems. My friend asked me if I would work for Keith as a turf accountant. I agreed; the loan went ahead. I now found a new connection with horses. Keith had been giving such generous odds, on each and every horse in any race, that no matter which horse came in the winner, Keith was on the losing side. My function was to ensure Keith kept the odds so that he would only lose on a favourite, break even on the second favourite and all the other runners would be winners for Keith if they won.

I confess to being somewhat nervous at the start. However, Keith proved to be a gentleman and we got on well together. We also started making money and slowly, but surely, Keith started to repay the loan. But it was slow and looked likely that it would take more time than I was prepared to give before the loan would be fully repaid.

I had been clerking with Keith for several months when I noticed a bundle of money in his safe. I asked Keith about it. He replied, "You don't want to know." I reminded him of his undertaking to his backer and let him know in no uncertain terms that I did need to know.

It transpired that a certain jockey was placing the money in Keith's safe as 'security' against his winning on a fancied horse in a race where the likely winner would come from only one of a couple of horses. These races were not major events but were confined to horses that had yet to enter the winner's enclosure. With such knowledge, the jockey's horse could be chalked up at better odds than those given by other bookies in the ring on race day. This meant that any money laid on that horse could then be bet on the other horse likely to win the race. Whilst I had grave reservations, I saw this as an opportunity to get out of my commitment sooner rather than later. The scam went ahead and we were suddenly making much more money than before and the debt was being rapidly reduced.

Like any good thing, it came to an abrupt end. One race day, the usual 'guarantee' was in the safe and there were only two likely contenders. Unknown to us, another jockey was in cahoots with another bookie, planning the same swindle on the other competitive horse. As the race was reaching the finishing post, there were the two jockeys pulling in their respective nags with the result that an absolute outsider came through and took the race. That was the end of that! We lost heavily. The debt was finally settled a few weeks later and I walked away.

I witnessed many other occasions when a 'dead cert' came in last for no apparent reason. I have seen serious punters go home in tears, probably from frustration.

One positive from my clerking days. I have never placed a bet on any horse again. If you must make a bet, put your money on a favourite with odds less than evens. Statistics show that nearly 75% of such horses make it to the winner's enclosure. I realise that you won't make huge profits this way, but your return, over a period of time, will be positive and not negative.

One last mention of Keith; he died of a heart attack in the middle of a game of squash. He was only 45 years old. (It seems so strange how many people I have had contact with, die an untimely death.)

10

Sport

I shan't pretend that I am one of the greats in sport. Suffice to say I have had my moments as I expect have most people. I recall being selected for the school shooting team in my first year at high school. I was a reasonably good shot and in the opening two inter-school matches, I managed to get two 'possibles'; (every shot in the dead centre of the target). I have never been able to repeat this achievement.

Rugby was the first sport in which I achieved some honours. I had played football at prep school, so had little idea of rugby. Lack of knowledge made me fearless as well as foolhardy. After a rocky start, I made progress. Starting with school colours; then on to Natal schools and eventually playing for several different provinces. I was somewhat tall at 6'2" to be a front rank but that is the position into which I was placed and it stuck. I recall playing in a game for national honours in Rhodesia in which I scored a try. Due to my size, I was unable to fit into the rugby jersey allotted to me and swapped with the other front rank in our team. As the jerseys were numbered he got the newspaper mention for scoring the try. Just my luck. I will add that he in fact was a far better player than I. His name: Andy McDonald. He made the Springbok team that year. On the upside, my employers did not find out that I was playing rugby when I should have been many miles away embarked on some geological exploration.

A few months after joining African Explosives, I was promoted to the financial section. Here, I learned that my boss was the chairman of a rugby club which had premier status. My boss had found out that I was a useful player and took little time in persuading me to start playing rugby again as I had stopped playing when I married Val.

At my first practice with the new club I was anxious to make a good impression and probably strutted towards the group of players for my introduction. Only two persons were vaguely familiar to me as I shook each one's hand on introduction. When I shook the hand of one of the two, he greeted me with a loud "Sing 'Laa'". I realised I had seen him before at the block of flats where I lived and he had heard my daily routine with my music teaching wife.

From rugby, I progressed to squash. I loved the game and was sorry to have to give it up when I developed a calcium spur on my heel. Absolute agony. I was just 50 years of age.

At that time one of my bookkeeping staff asked me to 'chaperone' her on a golf course. She was being pursued by one of our farming clients. I really did not have any enthusiasm for the outing. This was due to walking round golf courses with my father at a very tender age.

I could not believe what a fantastic environment golf courses are set out in. I got hooked, there and then, and still play. My handicap is barely ok at 18. I do have my moments from time to time. One of these I will now relate.

In 2015, I entered my club's seniors' championship. This is a stroke play competition. I did not have any unrealistic expectations. To me it was just another game. The third hole is a par 3 and is surrounded by bunkers. I put my first ball into the deepest bunker and struggled to get it out. When I did, on my ninth stroke, the ball sailed over the green into a bunker on the other side. I finally put the ball in the hole on stroke 16. On to the 7th hole, once again I found myself in a bunker. This time I managed to get down for 13 strokes. On two other holes, I managed 11 strokes and 8 strokes. This meant I had used 48 strokes on just four holes.

I persevered. Things could not get any worse; could they? On the 17th hole, also a par 3, I could not find my ball. With one hole to go I could not throw in the towel at this stage. I started the long walk back to the tee. One of the other players in my group asked me what ball I was playing. I informed him and he called me over to the pin. There was my ball in the cup. My first and only hole-in-one. My gross score for the round was 122 including my fluke.

I recently played in a major seniors' stableford competition at my golf club. We teed off in three-balls; Mike, Dennis and myself. Dennis struggles at the best of times and never looked like competing. After 9 holes, Mike had scored 17 points and I had 18. Considering the windy conditions, this was a fair effort. The last nine holes were a battle with neither of us gaining an upper hand. I dropped a shot towards the end and after we both parred the last two holes we had 38 points each. This meant I had lost to Mike on count-back. What neither of us realised was that 38 points was the winning score. I was delighted with my second place. When the result was announced by the club captain I was totally surprised to hear I had won the event and Mike was second. During the round, he had experienced a 'duff' shot which he reported on completing the round and was accordingly deducted the one stroke difference.

My sole reason for relating this story is to remind everyone that there are true sporting people in the world and winning at all costs is not always the case. I salute Mike for his honesty and hope that under similar circumstances I will be big enough to do the same.

There is an amusing golf story (not true) about a golfer playing at the Elephant Hills course at Victoria Falls. At the first hole, he came across a warthog grazing on the green. He looked to his caddy for help and was handed a shotgun. He fired and the warthog departed. At the next hole, he found a python wrapped around the flag on the green. Again, the caddy handed him the shotgun. After firing at the python it slithered off into the undergrowth. On the third hole our golfer found himself in a bunker. As he was about to play, a crocodile grabbed his trousers and started dragging the golfer to the nearby Zambesi river. The golfer shouted and screamed at his caddy for help. To no avail. In desperation, the golfer repeatedly hit the crocodile on the head with his golf club until he was eventually released. The golfer asked his caddy why he had not passed over the gun. The caddy replied, "Sir, you do not get a shot on this hole."

Though it is not yet regarded as a sport, I know that the powers that be are actively trying to have it classified as one. I refer to bridge which is my other area of some success.

It feels as if I have been playing bridge for ever. I only started playing competitive bridge after my first wife had joined a club in Harare. Before that, I played every Tuesday night for eight years with a group of friends some of which I still see here in England. The standard of our game was poor but, boy, did we have fun. We took turns in hosting the game. At one venue, the wife of our host gave us frozen egg sandwiches every time we played at his house. Egg sandwiches are not my favourite, but frozen egg sandwiches are disgusting. We took it in turns to send our host off to his kitchen so that we could dump the food out of the window where his dog would have a feast. We never let on.

On another occasion, I had made some 'excellent' mulberry wine. I decided to serve it to get a reaction from the players. Within an hour we were all smashed! The alcohol level must have been really high. I did overhear one comment. "This tastes like sh**. Please fill up my glass!" I never let on to the source or the origin of the wine. Suffice to say that the remaining four bottles were all consumed. Not surprisingly, I can't remember anything else of the night.

It was only when I joined a duplicate bridge club that I woke up to the fact that my knowledge of the game was very limited. Many years on, I find I am still learning and hopefully improving. While I cannot claim to have expert status I have had success at a reasonable county level. Some years back when I first came to England, I was fortunate to partner Christine whom I rate as the best partner I have had. She moved to France about eight years ago. My present bridge partner, Gill, is a good player and we have been top pair at our club for the past three years. I am sorry that I cannot get Wendy to play as I had so much enjoyment playing with Brenda, my late wife. She had me agreeing to a fine of £5 every time I criticised her play. (The amount of £5 was equivalent to Z$500.) On one occasion she made a mistake and I could not help myself. I opened my mouth again, and again, and again. Each time I spoke, Brenda added up the fine. By the time it reached £45 I knew I was on a hiding to nothing. I never once criticised her play after that.

In my humble opinion, playing duplicate bridge in team events is even more enjoyable than a 'pairs' game.

In my bachelor days, I shared digs with a pilot. Zack belonged to the Mount Hampden Flying Club. One day he invited me to have a flight with him. I met him at the airfield and was more than a little concerned to see we were going up in an ancient Tiger Moth. He gave me a flying cap and told me to indicate with my thumbs whether or not I was ok. Thumbs up obviously meant 'continue' while thumbs down meant 'return to base'. The cap barely covered my head and definitely ruled out any possibility of my hearing any instructions Zack might have for me.

We took off and the initial minutes were great. After we had reached a cruising height, Zack spoke to me over the intercom. I could not make out what he had said but presumed he was asking if I was happy to continue. I gave him the thumbs up. Next instant we went into a steep dive leaving my stomach way back at cruising level. He pulled the plane out of the dive when it seemed to me we were destined to crash. He then put the Tiger into a 'roll over the top'. We were now flying upside down. My stomach had now had enough and when Zack next spoke, I gave him a thumbs down sign. But, of course, we were flying upside down so my thumbs down, was a thumbs up as far as Zack was concerned.

For the next twenty minutes, Zack put the plane through a series of acrobatic manoeuvres that even a World War II ace would have been proud of. More rolls over the top; plenty of loop the loop and so on. By the time we landed I was a complete zombie and quite speechless. I had to head straight for the nearest washroom.

Another of my breathtaking adventures was 'shooting the rapids' on the Zambezi river just below the Victoria Falls. Nothing dramatic to report; just a wonderful experience.

11

Health

Touch wood! I feel I have been extremely fortunate as far as my health is concerned. As a child at boarding school, I naturally, came into contact with the usual diseases young children get. I contracted measles and chicken pox but escaped the others. I believe I am immune to mumps having escaped after having been in contact with mumps sufferers on many occasions.

I did have my tonsils removed at an early age and could have had an early untimely death. Following the operation, I was confined to bed for a few days. I became thoroughly bored and decided that I would 'camp' under the bed rather than spend any more time lying on top of it. When you go camping one of the first things you do is have a camp fire. Despite my great care and diligence my fire spread onto my mattress and sheets! I cannot remember what punishment I received, but as a 'sick child' I am sure my punishment was not too severe.

I have had one other operation. This happened a few years ago in England a few days before Christmas. I remember feeling ill. This feeling alone was unusual for me as I never, never feel ill. A visit to the doctor confirmed I had appendicitis. I was sent straight to A & E and was admitted some six hours later. By this time, my appendix had burst.

The incident has forever left me with a lasting good impression of the NHS. The doctors were good; the nurses were brilliant and the food, not bad at all. There was a minor problem: I was in a ward with six other elderly gentlemen all having stomach or bowel problems. As it was Christmas time, for supper, we were given the largest, smelliest Brussel sprout I have ever come across. The air quality in that ward that night was not good!

I have had one persistent problem for most of my later years. I found my feet ached walking round a golf course. My doctor prescribed Brufen, an anti-inflammatory for my condition. I took a little pink pill before a golf game without fail. One day my secretary came to my office and started giggling when I looked up at her. She suggested I take a look in the mirror as there was something drastically wrong. I literally staggered to the bathroom and had a huge fright when I saw my face. My lower jaw line had swollen to the size of a football. I discovered that the reason I could hardly get to the bathroom was because one of my testicles had become enlarged to the size of a melon. I had become allergic to Brufen.

Over the years I have tried various other anti-inflammatories; none particularly successful. Invariably I would have difficulty walking towards the end of 18 holes of golf. As this is usually a distance of 5 to 6 miles a game, I was not overly concerned. Then I discovered 'Rock Tape'. This is the coloured tape one sees athletes use on their various muscles. I placed a strip of the tape on the sole of each foot and found I could walk all day with hardly any pain. Amazing!

One last thing to mention regarding my health. About two years ago I experienced a severe pain on my right knee. The pain eased within a couple of weeks but I then had a pain in my right calf. Once this cleared up, the pain shifted to my Achilles. Eventually this too cleared, but the pain returned to my calf. Months later all the pain went but the muscle in my calf withered to nothing. It took an eternity to build the muscle back to a reasonable size. However, I now had a new lasting medical problem. My right leg between the calf and ankle started itching. The doctors put it down to an allergic reaction. I took various anti-inflammatories. I used several different creams to ease the itch. All to no avail. The itch just got worse and worse.

I was given an appointment to see a dermatologist but that was more than five months away. After nearly nine months I was now desperate. Short of cutting off my leg I had no idea what to do. Then, out of the blue came inspiration. I wrapped Rock Tape around my shin! The relief was immediate. I slept soundly for the first time in weeks. One week later I had not had even the slightest itch. I removed the tape and the blistered skin area had healed nicely. I understand the theory of the tape lies in its adhering to the skin, thus allowing blood to flow under the skin and, in so doing, clearing up infections etc.

I am not sure whether anyone will have found this of interest. Perhaps, just perhaps, it might give another person a fresh look at the possibilities.

One more word on the NHS. As an elderly person, I am given an annual flu jab. This last year, my flu jab was followed by a shingles jab in the other arm. I did not even know what shingles is. It did not take even a day for me to find out. My upper arms and chest came out in a severe rash and didn't stop itching for three weeks. Before the jabs, I was feeling quite good about my well-being. I still wonder why the doctor thought it necessary to give me a dose of shingles. I am still trying to solve the problem.

Good heath depends, to a great extent, on healthy eating. I expect there must be hundreds of different ideas on what constitutes a healthy diet. I am not about to give anyone my recipe for healthy living but I thoroughly enjoy cooking. I think my boarding school diet set me on a path of what not to eat as my lasting memory of boarding school was that all the food was tasteless.

I set about trying to make the meals I prepare to have plenty of taste; quality not quantity. One of my early disappointments came in my days as a geologist. I was responsible at one of the camps for organising the daily food and, on this occasion, preparing the evening meal. Of the six participants, five had to be taken to the local hospital with gastric problems. Only I escaped. The doctor was unable to determine the cause of everyone's discomfort, so no blame was put on me. Suffice to say from then on I was no longer allocated kitchen duties.

I also remember preparing a very tasty dish for Val, my first wife. I went to the kitchen for a second helping and was surprised on my return to the table to find Val had an empty plate. She declined another helping but congratulated me on a lovely meal. Two weeks later I was looking over the balcony railing when I saw a very strange mass of some thing or other on the ground several feet below. I soon discovered that it was Val's supper. No wonder she had emptied her plate so quickly. But what really hurt was the fact that not even the stray dogs and cats in the neighbourhood had finished it off.

Today, I have become a somewhat better cook and, as I am at home, undertake most of the cooking. Wendy does the party food; I do the rest. I must admit though, that no matter what I cook, be it meat or fish or something other, all my meals taste vaguely similar. It must be that lemon juice I put into almost everything I cook!! There are certain flavours that I find distasteful. One of these is the herb, coriander. If you have ever been to Cyprus, you will understand. Everything I ever ate while dining out there seemed to be smothered with coriander.

I am not particularly fond of food with Eastern flavours and this includes curries. My family all adore curry. Wendy and I once went to a charity dinner and sure enough the starters, main course and desert were all Indian dishes. The hostess of the event had been warned of my culinary dislikes and prevailed on the chef to prepare something 'special' for me. I was served dried up chicken nuggets and burnt chips; perhaps the worst meal I have ever had to pay for. (Bring back the curry!)

Epilogue

I have come to the end of my ramblings. I am positive there are stories I should have remembered which are now lost to me, probably for ever. I must confess to have indulged myself in believing anyone else will find some interest in these memoirs. I hope so. Even if this is not the case, I have left my children and their offspring an account of my life of which they have little knowledge.

I am not sure how I wish my life to end. I do know I don't want to live to an age where I cannot look after myself. Call it independence. I have a standing joke with Wendy that I want to swim in the Mediterranean, probably in Greece, and head for deep waters, never to be seen again.

If I have any disappointment to reflect on, it has to be around the matter of 'fairness'. I have trouble reconciling religion and the existence of God, when so many happenings in our world strike me as being unfair. Young children contracting cancer is one example. And there are so, so many others. I leave it to you to ponder from your personal experiences.

With hindsight, I count myself to have been so fortunate in the paths that my fatalistic philosophy has taken me. Sure; things have happened to me which I regard as unfair; but so what. Regrets are few; perhaps I could have been a better husband to my four wives. I shall choose to blame my shortcomings on my upbringing and leave it there. After all, I have to live with myself, albeit, even for a few more years.

I have put the name of 'Reflections' to this work. Perhaps it should be entitled 'Reflections and Confessions.'